TRADE AND ENVIRONMENT IN THAILAND

An Emerging Economy

KAKALI MUKHOPADHYAY

SERIALS PUBLICATIONS
NEW DELHI

First Published - 2007

ISBN: 81-8387-090-2

Published by

SERIALS PUBLICATIONS
4830/24, Prahlad Street, Ansari Road
Darya Ganj, New Delhi-110002 (India)
Phone : 23245225. Fax : 91-11-23272135
E-mail: serials@satyam.net.in

To my mother

for her unfailing support

Contents

Preface

The complex interrelationship between trade and environment has become a focal point for international as well as national policy makers. Standard economic theory assumes that free trade leads to a win-win situation of all players participating in international trade. However, free trade has an overall positive or negative impact on the environment. It offers both benefits and costs to environmental quality depending on a number of factors including the existence of optimal environmental protection measures, the level of economic and technological development, and the level of environmental awareness. Environmentalists argue that free trade is responsible for environmental problems because free trade is likely to increase production and consumption of environmentally unfriendly goods and services leading to high pollution and environmental degradation. So trade can be in conflict with environmental protection.

The past 15 years have seen an increasing debate over the linkages between trade and environmental regulations. From this debate two conflicting hypotheses......pollution haven and factor endowment ...... have emerged. First, the pollution haven hypothesis (PHH) suggests that the developed countries impose tougher environmental policies than the developing countries, resulting in distortion of existing patterns of comparative advantage. So the polluting industries shift operations from the developed to the developing countries; developing countries thus become "pollution havens." The second hypothesis, the factor endowment hypothesis (FEH) predicts, trade liberalisation will result in trade patterns consistent with the Heckscher-Ohlin-Vanek (HOV) theory of comparative advantage based on factor endowment differentials. Rich countries are well endowed with capital. Since capital-intensive goods are often also pollution-intensive, factor-endowment theories of international trade assume that rich countries specialize in polluting goods. Thus the manifestation of the PHH is in direct conflict with the FEH.

This issue is of great concern among economists, environmentalists and world bodies like WTO, but there is no consensus. The review of the literature also suggests that the empirical evidence is still far from clear (Copeland and Taylor, 2004). The methodologies employed to test the hypothesis are widely varied so are the results. Hence, the biggest challenge in front of us is to promote liberal trade while maintaining and strengthening protection of the environment. Towards this end, the present volume has made a modest effort to address the current debate. It attempts to assess the magnitude of the effects of trade liberalization on the environment in context of Thailand, a newly industrializing economy.

The Thai economy has evidenced rapid growth in recent years, and is viewed as an example of economic success in the region. This growth has largely been led by increased participation in international trade, especially a marked increase in exports. The intense economic and largely industrial development, significant changes in trade pattern and the production technology have important implications for the environment and also serious consequences for the future of the Thai economy. Thus Thailand is a good laboratory for assessing the impact of trade on the environment by testing the above mentioned two hypotheses.

The objective of the present study is to estimate the impact of Thailand's trade with rest of the world and exclusively OECD on CO_2, SO_2 and NOx emissions from fossil fuel combustion during 1980 to 2000. Firstly, the study measures the pollution terms of trade reflecting Thailand's environmental gains or losses from trade. Secondly, it finds out the relevance of the factor endowment hypothesis. Finally, it examines the implications of foreign direct investment on the environment. To identify the trade impact on environment the study has calibrated models based on Input-Output framework.

I hope this effort will make a modest contribution to trade and environment debate and provide some direction for trade and environmental policies. Scholars and policy makers of the newly industrialized economies and the countries embarking on major liberalization programme may find the book useful.

Acknowledgements

I am pleased to acknowledge academicians, policy makers, and several government organisations in Thailand who have made major contributions towards completion of this work, the content of which is an outcome of a research work funded by Ford Foundation. The findings of this work have been presented in various seminars in Thailand (Trade and Environment Division, UN-ESCAP; School of Environment Resources and Development, AIT; TDRI-Thailand Environment Forum; International Institute for Trade and Development) and in India (Indira Gandhi Institute of Development Research and Madras School of Economics). Thanks are due to the participants of these seminars for their comments and suggestions which have contributed to the improvement of the book.

I gratefully acknowledge Asian Scholarship Foundation (Ford Foundation) for funding me to carry out the study in Thailand. My special gratitude goes to Dr. Lourdes G. Salvador (Executive Director, ASF) for her continuous support and encouragement. Thanks are also due to Ms. Somkamol Yongkrittaya for her excellent cooperation during the fellowship tenure. This study would not have been completed without assistance and immense support from various government offices (National Economic and Social Development Board; National Statistical Organisation; Ministry of Commerce, Customs Department, Pollution Control Department, Ministry of Natural Resource and Environment and Bank of Thailand) and institutes (Thailand Development Research Institute, Thailand Environment Institute) of Thailand. The author is thankful to the trade and environment group of UN-ESCAP, Bangkok, especially Lorenzo Santucci for valuable comments. I acknowledge AIT for extending all facilities to my research work. Especially, I am indebted to Prof. R.M. Shrestha (SERD, Energy, AIT) for providing opportunity to carry out the study during the period of ASF fellowship (November 2004-September 2005). I express my sincere thanks to Prof. Jayanta Bandyopadhyay (Coordinator, Centre for Development and Environment Policy, Indian Institute of Management Calcutta) for being a source of inspiration. I am also deeply indebted to Prof. Debesh Chakraborty (Department of Economics, Jadavpur University, Calcutta, India) for providing helpful comments, constructive suggestions and insights while preparing the manuscript and refining the text.

This book would not have appeared without the support provided by IIMC in general and CDEP in particular for its completion.

Finally, I like to acknowledge Prof. Paul Thomassin (Department of Agricultural Economics, McGill University, Québec, Canada) for his financial support and encouragement to complete the monograph.

Kakali Mukhopadhyay

Department of Agricultural Economics
McGill University, Quebec, Canada
&
Centre for Development and Environment Policy,
Indian Institute of Management Calcutta
Calcutta, India

1

Introduction

Trade and environment is a multifaceted issue. The interrelationship between trade and the environment has become a pressing concern across the globe. There are both threats and opportunities in this relationship for countries, local communities and firms pursuing economic development and environmental protection. How changing trade regimes affect the environment and how stricter environmental regulations (as well as a general increase in environmental awareness and concern) affect trade is a serious concern among economists, environmentalists, policy makers and world bodies like WTO.

A policy of trade liberalization is often suggested as a means of stimulating economic growth in developing countries. Trade liberalization consists of policies aimed at opening up the economy to foreign investment and lowering trade barriers in the form of tariff reduction. On the other hand, increasing economic openness has led to concerns about possible detrimental effects on the environment. It may lead to more pollution either as a result of relocation of polluting industries from countries with strict environmental policy or due to increased production in dirty industries.

There is an emerging consensus in the environmentalist community opposing free trade (Drake-Brockman & Anderson, 1994).They argue that free trade is responsible for environmental problems because free trade is likely to increase production and consumption of environmentally unfriendly goods and services leading to high pollution and environmental degradation.

The recent greening of world politics has brought forward many claims as to the effects of trade and hence trade policy on the environment. Environmentalists have also made suggestions for government intervention to slow the degradation of the natural environment, which will not only affect the implementing country but also trade, environment and welfare of other countries as well (Audley, 1997).

TRADE AND ENVIRONMENT ISSUES

The trade and environment arguments cover two intrinsically different but closely linked types of issues: the analytical issues and the negotiation-related issues. The analytical issues refer to the inquiries into the causal link between trade policy and environment and/or environmental quality. The negotiations related issues mean the subjects of controversies on how to reconcile the present and potential conflicts between environmentally motivated policy goals and international trade rules. At present, the negotiation related issues are of utmost interest. However, the analytical issues are also important, usually a topic of economic research. The result of the analyses may significantly affect the orientation of the negotiation- related issues. Table 1.1 presents a structure of trade and environment issues.

TRADE AND ENVIRONMENT: FURTHER DISCUSSION

Trade theory suggests that for a small country, in the absence of market imperfections, the use of trade barriers creates market distortions that reduce overall welfare. Environmental concerns involve externalities that cannot be captured by market forces alone. In this situation, the use of trade control measures would be more effective to achieve environmental goals. On the other hand, the use of trade measures for environmental purposes has been viewed as disguised protectionism. The issues, however, have become more complex and deeper.

Table 1.1
A Typology of Trade-Environment Issues

......of the analytical type	1. Impact of trade on environment (a) impact of type trade liberalization on the environment (b) impact of environment related trade measure on the environment 2. Impact of environmental regulations on trade pattern(or competitiveness)
......of the negotiation related type	1. Trade measures for environmental purposes: relationship with trade rules (a) trade measures for domestic environment preservation (b) trade measures relating to transnational pollution (c) trade measures relating to the global environment (d) trade measures on inappropriate environmental policies of other countries (e) export of hazardous products and wastes 2. trade effects of domestic environmental measures 3. others

Source: United Nations Publication (2003), Environment and Trade.

It has also been demonstrated that free trade maximizes the efficiency of resource allocation by channeling economic activities to least-cost producers. It thus produces a given level of output at the least cost. If natural and environmental resources are efficiently priced, the global output resulting from free trade is also produced at the least environmental cost. Free trade maximizes social welfare. For example, countries with high levels of agricultural protection use more than ten times as much chemical fertilizers and pesticides per hectare as countries with low level protection. In this case, trade liberalization would reduce the use of agrochemicals and hence environmental degradation in protectionist countries significantly and increase it marginally in low protection countries. This results in overall gains in environmental protection and sustainability. If, however, there are market failures or policy failures the resources are misallocated and removal of barriers to trade may worsen this misallocation.

Under such conditions, freer trade would not maximize social welfare. There would still be efficiency gains (positive effects) but there would also be welfare losses as wasteful resource depletion and environmental degradation are aggravated (negative effects). The net effect on social welfare would depend on the relative magnitude of the positive and negative effects. Failure to internalise environmental costs at the national level can also contribute to transboundary and global environmental problems. At this stage it needs to be discussed what the impact of trade on the environment is.

Trade flows and trade liberalization have at least six types of physical and economic impacts on environment and development: (a) Scale effects; (b) Income effects; (c) Structural or Composition effects; (d) Product effects; (e) Technology diffusion; and (f) Regulatory effects (Townsend & Ratnayake,2000). Each of this is examined below.

Scale effects

The positive scale effect occurs when increased trade induces better environmental protection through economic growth and policy development. It stimulates product composition and technology shifts that cause less pollution per unit of output. The negative effects can be reflected when increased trade leads to more pollution without compensating product, technology or policy developments. Negative scale effects are more pronounced where there are market failures.

Income effects

The gains from trade and trade-driven economic growth result in substantial income increases which impact the environment in a variety of ways. First, higher incomes result in both higher levels of consumption and associated environmental externalities, and in higher willingness to pay for environmental improvement, and associated increases in both private and public environmental expenditures. There is considerable empirical evidence that environmental quality is income elastic, in the sense that increases in income result in more than proportionate increases in environmental expenditures (Townsend & Ratnayake, 2000). Second, economic growth makes more resources available for environmental protection, and raises environmental quality in a country's list of priorities. Governments increase environmental expenditures both in absolute terms and as a percentage of GDP. This is happening in all the newly industrializing countries (e.g. China, South Korea, Mexico and Brazil). The reverse is also true. When income growth slows down environmental expenditures tend to fall more than proportionally. Third, trade liberalization may help reduce the pressures due to poverty on the environment through the encroachment of natural resources. On the other hand, poor people are further marginalized due to global competition without access to technology, capital and other means to compete. Encroachment and degradation of natural resources (forest, pastures, fisheries, public lands) are likely to intensify. Trade liberalization may reinforce the vicious circle between poverty and environmental degradation, especially when open access resources are being exploited for exports. Finally, economic growth may result in reform of environmental policies and enactment of new laws and regulations and new institutions to enforce them.

Studies of the relationship between income levels and environmental degradation, not controlling for scale and structural change effects, found an inverted U-shape relationship, especially for localized effects. (Grossman and Krueger, 1995, Panayotou 1997). At low income levels (early stages of development), income growth is associated with higher levels of environmental degradation until a turning point is reached beyond which further income increases result in environmental improvement. This finding is known as the Environmental Kuznets Curve. This suggests that environmental degradation is a "growing up" problem to be overcome through rapid economic growth rather than through targeted environmental policies. To the extent that liberalized trade pushes economic growth and raises per capita income, any restrictions on trade or diversions of resources away from export-led growth slow down the transition to a positive income-environment relationship (Townsend & Ratnayke, 2000).

Structural or Composition effects

Globalization in general and freer trade in particular changes industrial structure more in line with a country's comparative advantage. In the absence of market and policy failures, the composition of output under free trade would be better suited to a country's environmental resource endowment than under austerity. Controlling for scale effects and for stage of development, trade liberalization tends to make the structure of the economy less pollution-intensive to speed up the transition from resource extraction and processing to light manufacturing and eventually services. Since most developing countries are more richly endowed in low-cost labor than any other factor of production, trade liberalization tends to shift labor-intensive activities to developing countries. Indeed, Hettige, Lucas and Wheeler (1992) found that toxic intensity increased more rapidly in inward-looking developing countries, while outward-oriented, high-growth developing countries had a slowly increasing or declining toxic intensity of manufacturing. They found that highly protected economies had experienced rapid growth in capital-intensive smokestack sectors, while more open economies had experienced high growth in less pollution-intensive, more labor-intensive activities.

Developing countries may also have considerable natural resource endowments and income-constrained demand for environmental quality. The extent to which trade liberalization would contribute to sustainable development, under these conditions, depends critically on whether environmental assets are properly valued, and these values are somehow been taken into account by world markets. Otherwise, trade liberalization may shift the production structure towards increased specialization in unsustainable activities.

Product effects

The product effects of trade liberalisation are determined by how the removal of barriers to trade changes the product composition of trade. Positive product effects deriving from increased trade in environmentally friendly goods and the transfer of environmental technologies and services will help offset the potential negative scale and structural effects arising from freer trade (for example, biodegradable containers). More trade in environmentally damaging products can be treated as negative effects (e.g. hazardous wastes).

Technology diffusion

Liberalized trade facilitates the diffusion of products, technologies and processes across borders. The environmental impact of this diffusion depends on the characteristics of the products and technologies. The trade in products that has adverse effect on the environment (such as toxic chemicals, hazardous waste, endangered species and disease bearing pests) is strictly regulated or prohibited by international conventions. A very important channel through which globalization impacts the environment is the trade in environmentally preferred "producer" and "consumer" goods. The positive effects can be measured from reducing pollution per unit of product (e.g., precision farming that reduces excess fertilizer use). The negative effects generate from the spread of "dirty" technologies, (e.g., highly toxic and persistent pesticides) through trade channels.

The global market for environmental goods and services is around $300 billion annually and is increasing rapidly (OECD 1996). Trade liberalization expands the potential market for both more efficient capital equipment and "cleaner" production technologies on the production side and "greener" products, such as organic foods, low-emission vehicles and recyclables, on the consumption side. While other dimensions of globalization, such as investment, intellectual property rights and economic integration, have technology implications that impact the environment. Three quarters of all technology transfer arise from trade flows (OECD 1994), especially the trade in machinery and equipment, which amounts to almost 40 per cent of total global trade (UN 1996).

These trade flows result in diffusion of more efficient and cleaner technologies. Almost 80 per cent of the global trade in machinery and equipment comes from developed countries and about a third is imported by developing countries (UN 1996). Technology diffusion also takes place through the trade in services such as engineering and consulting services and technology licensing.

Liberalized trade contributes not only to technology diffusion and transfer but also to technological progress through economies of scale, enhanced incentives to innovate and less duplication of research and development efforts due to fewer protectionist barriers (Grossman and Helpman 1995).

The question arises—does the trade-induced generation and diffusion of technology benefits or harms the environment? The technology-environment relationship is a complex one consisting of both demand and supply factors and policy effects. On the demand side, pressures by regulators, customers, shareholders and the community drive firms to demand technology with environmental characteristics such as "cleaner" production technology and pollution-abatement equipment. While regulatory and community pressures usually aim at process characteristics, customers pressure is directed towards product characteristics. Studies of firm behavior in developed countries tend to find regulatory pressure as the most potent driver of environmentally-preferred technologies (Henriques and Sadorsky, 1996) while studies of firm behavior in developing countries tend to find community pressures as the most important determinant of firms' environmental behavior (Pargal and Wheeler, 1996; Panayotou *et al.* 1997).

On the supply side, environment-related technological change is driven by abatement costs and the ability of innovating firms to benefit from environmental damage mitigation and to appropriate the benefits from innovation with wider applications. According to Johnstone (1997), in addition to these factors, the level of industrial research and development is likely to be an important factor in the supply of environment-relevant technological innovations.

Regulatory effects

The regulatory effects of trade liberalization on the environment arise from (a) improved environmental policies, standards and enforcement in response to economic growth from increased trade; (b) environmental measures included in trade agreements; and (c) relaxation of existing environmental policies due to specific trade pressures or restrictions on environmental policies by trade agreements. With regard to the first effect above, World Bank research based on data from 145 countries has found a positive association between economic growth and environmental regulation and security of property rights. With regard to the second effect, NAFTA demonstrates how trade liberalization can serve as a catalyst for improvements in both the level and the enforcement of environmental regulations. Trade agreements in general may promote harmonization of environmental standards and influence policies towards environmental subsidies and environment-related fiscal and trade measures. While the multilateral trading system encourages the use of international standards, and allows for higher levels of environmental protection, there is a widespread concern that trade liberalization and the resulting zeal for competitiveness would "drag down" environmental standards in a race towards the bottom.

IMPACT OF ENVIRONMENTAL REGULATIONS ON TRADE PATTERN

As countries become more concerned about environmental degradation they are adopting a number of measures in the form of environmental regulation to minimize the damage caused to the environment.

Above all the most pressing consensus is the migration of 'dirty' industries to less strictly regulated countries. In this context two contrasting views can be mentioned. On the one hand, environment is treated as another factor of production included in the cost procedure and thus stringent environmental regulations raise cost of production. This is known as classical comparative advantage trade perspective. According to other view, known as neo-technology trade perspective, it is argued whether stringent environmental regulations resulted in migration of dirty industries to locations with lax regulations. To evaluate whether firms locate in countries to take advantage of lax environmental regulations it is necessary to look carefully at the quantitative importance of the different factors that determine location decisions. It involves a number of factors, including the cost of labour, access to markets, social and political conditions in the country concerned, the infrastructure facilities in the country concerned and the regulatory framework. The last includes environmental regulations but they are only part of the set of regulations. A lot of evidence exists to the effect that investors look not only at current regulations but also at the stability of the regulatory framework (how frequently governments change the rules). Studies have shown that these decisions are most influenced by such factors as labour costs, access to markets and the existence of a developed industrial base (Wheeler and Mody, 1992).

From the implication of the above discussion, some controversial hypotheses have generated i.e. pollution havens versus pollution haloes hypothesis and Porter hypothesis; industrial flight/race-to-the-bottom and race-to-the-top and factor endowment hypothesis. These hypotheses are all linked with one another. The pollution haven hypothesis (PHH), states that change in environmental regulations can distort existing patterns of comparative advantage. In the developed world the costs of complying with environmental regulations appear to be increasing steadily. Since the stringency of environmental regulations increases with income and economic development (Dasgupta et al. 1995) the PHH assumes that developing countries possess a comparative advantage in pollution-intensive production. Thus "pollution havens" arise. On the whole according to "pollution havens" hypothesis extended from comparative advantage perspective, in order to attract investment, less developed countries through lax environmental regulations create comparative advantage in pollution-intensive industries. More specifically, the countries with laxer standards–who are mostly the less developed countries engaging in environmental dumping- seek to attract more investments or try to get higher share from the world market by producing and exporting pollution-intensive goods. On the other hand, the countries with tougher standards import the pollution-intensive goods from these countries (Frankel and Rose, 2001).

Additionally, "industry flight" implies migration of polluting industries to locations with lax environmental regulations, and hence, gives birth to "race-to-the-bottom" hypothesis. This indicates worsening procedure of environmental standards in the host country. According to the "race-to-the-top" hypothesis raising environmental standards, related with the "pollution haloes" argument, indicate that foreign firms pull environmental standards upward by using better management practices. Industry flight phenomenon mainly depends on the concept of production. The differences in production costs among countries will encourage the industries to relocate their plants in a country providing low cost. Accordingly, lenient environmental regulations that a country impose, will give birth to low cost situation. "Porter hypothesis" extended from neo-technology trade perspective, implies that stringent environmental regulations stimulate the innovations and make the regulatory country net exporter of the newly developed environmental technologies.

Static view of environmental regulation suggests that there is a trade-off between social benefits and private costs as well as between ecology and economy. According to dynamic one, new paradigm as developed by Porter and Linde (1995), environmental standards can trigger innovation that may partially or more than fully offset the costs of complying with them. On the other hand, Palmer et al. (1995) denied the mentioned trade-off, and suggested several instances where environmental regulations operate on pollution firms' advantage. Jaffe and Palmer (1997) put forth three extensions of the hypothesis for consideration. First one, the "narrow version" implies that certain types of environmental regulations stimulate innovation without clear empirical implications. Second, "weak version" states that regulations stimulate certain types of innovation, whereas the last one, "strong version" suggests that regulation induces innovation whose benefits exceed its costs making it socially desirable.

The above discussed hypotheses are generated mainly from the different role of environmental regulation and its complexities in different countries.

Another motive for trade can be captured in the factor endowment hypothesis (FEH). It argues that trade liberalisation will result in trade patterns consistent with the Heckscher-Ohlin-Vanek (HOV) theory of comparative advantage based on factor endowment differentials. Rich countries are typically well endowed with physical capital. Since capital-intensive goods are often also pollution-intensive[1], factor-endowment theories of international trade predict that rich countries specialize in polluting goods. However, rich countries might have a higher willingness to pay for environmental quality and thus set higher environmental standards.

From the general premise that pollution intensive goods are relatively capital intensive (Antweiler et al. 2001, Cole, Elliott and Azar 2001), it is assumed that pollution-intensive (also known as "dirty") industries will relocate production from countries in the relatively labour abundant South to those in the relatively capital abundant North. Thus, the manifestation of the PHH is in direct conflict with the FEH.

From the above discussion of these hypotheses the main concern lies with the nature of environmental regulation either lax or strict. The laxity of environmental regulation in international trade creates one country better off putting other worse. A number of measures are being implemented to protect trade and environment simultaneously at the national as well as global level.

On the one hand eco-labeling or environmental management certification is aimed at protecting trade at the national and international label. Simultaneously international trade laws such as CITES and Cartegena protocol or Stockholm convention are emphasizing on maintaining the environmental quality.

New environmental regulation instruments are being developed (for example, environmental packaging, eco-labeling and recycling requirements) in order to encourage life cycle management of products. A set of pressures arises from the various programmes to label goods as environmentally friendly known as environmental labeling programmes. There are a number of different labeling schemes that come under this general title. The schemes included range from single criteria labels (recyclability, degradability, and so on) to others based on a life cycle assessment of the product's environmental assessment. A number of developed countries, as well as some developing countries, have such schemes.

Even though these policies are preferable to less direct trade policies, the potential remains for these policies which may result in protectionist outcomes. Eco-labeling provides information on standards that affect the characteristics of the final product. This is valuable to consumers. The market prices should reflect the differences in their environmental characteristics. The Geneva-based International Organization for Standardization (ISO) has established definitions and principles for developing each type. **Type I** (ISO 14024) labels compare products with others within the same category, awarding labels to those that are environmentally preferable through their whole life cycle. The criteria are set by an independent body and monitored through a certification, or auditing, process. **Type II** (ISO 14021) labels are environmental claims made about goods by their manufacturers, importers or distributors. **Type III** (ISO 14025) labels list a menu of a product's environmental impacts throughout its life cycle. They are similar to nutrition labels on food products that detail fat, sugar or vitamin contents. The information categories can be set by industrial sector or by independent bodies (UNEP, 2005).

Environmental management certification schemes assess a company's overall handling of environmental issues. Unlike ecolabels, these schemes do not imply anything about the environmental impacts of companies' products. Rather, they require companies to follow preset environmental principles and guidelines as they conduct business. Although some are more rigid than others, the requirements in such voluntary schemes are flexible and open to interpretation, and are generally less contentious than eco-labelling schemes.

The ISO 14001 environmental management system standard is one such scheme at the international level. ISO 14001 helps companies track, understand and improve their environmental management. To the extent that they are widely used, both ecolabels and EM (environmental management) should create environmental benefits. But they may also create problems, both of principle and of process, at the international level. The international structure of environmental management is dynamic. The various regimes address a wide variety of issues, ranging from toxic substances to endangered species, from air pollution to biodiversity (UNEP, 2005).

Whereas environmental standards can properly be set at the national level for impacts that are confined to national boundaries, the same does not apply when the domain of the impact is international, or even global. In the case of such issues as greenhouse gases, ozone-depleting substances (ODSs) or the conservation of threatened species international agreements are essential. These suggest specific actions to address the environmental problems that arise, and specify how the responsibility for the actions is to be divided up between nations.

Restrictions in trade are central to other international agreements, such as the Basel Convention on Trade in Hazardous Substances, and the Convention on Trade in Endangered Species(CITES). The key MEAs are : 1) Convention on International Trade in Endangered Species of Wild Fauna and Flora (CITES)—1973; 2) Vienna Convention for the Protection of the Ozone Layer—1985 and Montreal Protocol on Substances that Deplete the Stratospheric Ozone Layer—1987; 3) Basel Convention on the Control of Transboundary Movement of Hazardous Wastes and their Disposal—1992; 4) Convention on Biological Diversity—1992; and Cartagena Protocol on Biosafety—2000; 5) United Nations Framework Convention on Climate Change (UNFCCC)—1992, Kyoto Protocol to the United Nations Framework Convention on Climate Change—1997; 6) Rotterdam Convention on the Prior Informed Consent Procedure for Certain Hazardous Chemicals and Pesticides in International Trade (PIC)—1998 and 7) Stockholm Convention on Persistent Organic Pollutants (POPs)—2001(UNEP, 2005).

Nonetheless, while various studies might offer conflicting and/or inconclusive empirical results (see Chapter 2), clearer implications can at least be derived about the relationship between trade and environmental policies. This is that there should be no conflict between good economic policy and good environmental policy, between trade and environmental management. Good economic policy should not prevent the adoption and implementation of good environmental policy, and vice versa. To be sure, ideally, good economic policies and good environmental policies should both be present in order to attain optimum welfare. This is when goods and resources are properly priced and the market would work more efficiently, leading to optimum welfare. This argument is often overlooked in the discussion on trade and environment linkages.

The question is what is good-enough policy in the first place? What does a good environmental policy imply? Generally, it is one that leads to correct pricing of environmental resources, i.e., one that reflects relative scarcities and value to society. Hence, just as in the case of capital and labor, the relative price of environmental resources depends on relative factor endowments. If one country has a lower environmental standard than another, it could simply be a true reflection of the country's absorptive capacity, and not necessarily evidence of a "race to the bottom" or existence of pollution havens. Then again, there could be synergy between trade and environmental regulation. Openness to trade could lead to better environmental regulation (this is besides the possible positive income effects). Conversely, good environmental regulation could benefit trade.

However the debate over the linkages between trade and environment will remain and could become more complex in the future arising from increased global and regional integration.

In view of the above discussions a more in depth analysis and empirical evidence is necessary to draw conclusions for policy developments on these controversial issues. The present volume is aimed at this. It is considering Thailand one of the rapidly developing economies as a case study due to combination of factors given below.

WHY THAILAND

The Thai economy has evidenced rapid growth in recent years, and is viewed as an example of economic success in the south and south East Asian countries. The average annual growth rate between 1980 and 2004 is around 7 per cent. Thailand enjoyed its highest economic growth, averaging 9.1 per cent per annum during 1986-96. It can be considered the most prosperous time of the Thai economy. This growth has largely been led by increased participation in international trade, especially a marked increase in exports. The Thai exports have increased significantly by 45% (1980-85), 342% by 1990, 955% by 1995 & a staggering 2406% by 2003(Bank of Thailand, Quarterly Bulletin, various issues). Few countries in the world could claim this kind of dramatic growth in any sector of their economies.

With the rapid growth of Thailand's trade over the past 15 years, the composition of Thailand's exports has changed significantly. In 1985, 53% of the values of Thailand's exports were made up of agricultural & agro based industrial products. By the year 2004 only 8% came from agricultural products. More than 80% of the value of exports came from manufacturing and services. The big success story for Thailand has been the very rapid growth of manufacturing in the electronics sector, particularly computers, computer modules and integrated circuits with the increasing world demand. The Thai trade performance has changed considerably which is reflected in the sector of production and consumption. In the later half of the 1990s the situation started changing towards more capital intensive industry from labour intensive because of shifting of the trade towards more emerging industries. This diversification of exports was successfully supported and encouraged by the investment promotion activities of the Board of Investment (BOI), Thailand which attracted foreign capital to few selected export sectors. There is a huge inflow of FDI in Thailand primarily from Japan and USA and it is also boosting the exports.

To enhance export growth and sustain the international market the Thai government has also initiated several trade policies followed by important measures. Simultaneously Thailand implemented several laws and regulations to combat the environmental problems.

These changes in Thailand's trade pattern and also the role of FDI have important implications for the environment and the use of energy and other resources in the economy.

What happens to Thailand's environment in a liberalized trade regime is a matter of research. The current book attempts to study the interrelationship between trade and the environment focusing on Thailand.

OUTLINE OF THE STUDY

The literature on trade and the environment is surveyed in Chapter 2. This survey serves several purposes. The empirical estimation of the theory so far developed in the trade and environment literature is covered at national and international level. In this connection the survey also captures the debate originated from trade and environment relationship like pollution haven and factor endowment hypotheses. The literature on input-output method covering trade and environment work is also presented.

Chapter 3 introduces the structure of the Thai economy. It basically explains the economic growth —how it is achieved and other relevant indicators like trade and industrial growth. It discusses the growth of the manufacturing sector, its export and import, different industrial and trade policies taken so far in different plan period. Finally the chapter explains the environmental problems and policies in Thailand.

Chapter 4 develops the model for the study and data source for the empirical work. The model is based on input-output methodology, which is suitably modified for the purpose of the study. Three models have been presented. Model 1 explains the pollution haven hypothesis by considering the Hecksher-Ohlin assumption. This model has further been extended by relaxing this assumption. Factor endowment part is presented in model 2 and the impact of foreign direct investment on the environment is captured in model 3. The data sources are discussed according to their requirements in estimating three models.

Chapter 5 is devoted to the results and discussion on Pollution Haven Hypothesis based on model 1. The chapter also provides various reasons for the results.

Chapter 6 presents the results and analysis on factor endowment hypothesis based on model 2. It also offers explanations for the findings.

Chapter 7 discusses the role of foreign direct investment in Thailand which is one of the main drivers of the country's economic growth. The impacts of FDI on the environment with empirical results based on model 3 are also assessed.

Chapter 8 presents a summary and major conclusions derived from the study and some directions of future research. It also recommends several policy options to achieve the objectives of gains from trade while protecting the environment.

NOTE

1. An attempt has been made by Mani and Wheeler (1998) to link pollution intensity with capital and labour intensity of goods on the basis of the work of Hettige and others (1995). Emission intensity (emission per unit of output) has been calculated and the sectors that rank high on actual emission intensity. To determine high-ranking sectors by this criterion the authors have used detailed emissions intensities by medium for manufacturing in the United States by three digit standard industrial classification (SIC level) computed by the World Bank in collaboration with the United States Environmental Protection Agency and the United States census bureau (Hettige et al., 1995). They have computed average sectoral rankings for air pollutants. They have found that the following sectors which rank high are pollution-intensive industries: iron and steel, non-ferrous metal, nonmetallic mineral products, miscellaneous petroleum, coal products, pulp and paper, petroleum refineries, industrial chemicals and other chemicals, wood products and glass products. In addition, they have estimated the capital intensity of these dirty industries and found that dirty industries are relatively intensive in capital because capital intensity is substantially higher in the dirty sectors with an average ration around 2:1 for capital output and investment output. Following the criteria they have identified that iron and steel, metal products and chemical products are highly capital intensive as well as pollution intensive. They have also found that the clean sectors are about 40 per cent more labour intensive on average.

2

Review of Literature

Interactions between trade and the environment have already been a subject of academic discussions and notable empirical analyses. The literature in this field is growing. Various works attempt to provide empirical evidence about these linkages. And not surprisingly, findings are mixed, if not conflicting. It has produced an increasingly greater need for a careful and balanced assessment of the issues involved and the challenges they pose to policy makers.

The present effort thus attempts to provide a more comprehensive survey as per as possible of this area. The approach taken has been to evaluate studies linking trade and environment. The topics and issues have been organized to include: (1) the nature of macroeconomic impacts, (2) patterns of trade and comparative advantage, (3) terms of trade, (4) patterns of production and consumption, (5) linkages between trade, environment and the economy, (6) pollution redeployment to developing countries, (7) environmental degradation, and (8) factor rewards.

Already there are various approaches applied in this field such as computable general equilibrium model, international trade model, input-output model, welfare analysis model, game theoretic model, optimization model, spatial GIS model, and econometric model. Since our study is based on Input-Output framework the survey will focus separately literature on trade and environment using Input-Output model.

MACROECONOMIC IMPACTS

In this section the macro economic impacts basically cover income, employment, other variables, balance of trade and impact on sustainable development.

The impacts of domestic environmental control policies on national income are first assessed by D'Areg (1971). Using the trade model, D'Areg has estimated domestic income effects resulting from changes in export prices due to the imposition of domestic environmental policies. He has found that the impact on domestic income stemming from international feedback effects is negative and has come primarily through impact multipliers. Siebert et al. (1980) also analyze the effects of domestic environmental policies on national income using general equilibrium models. They conclude that environmental policy will reduce resources used in an emission-intensively producing sector and in production activities in both sectors. Many other studies reveal the negative effects of environmental policies on national income [Manne and Richels (1991a), (1991b), and (1992); Manne (1992); Dervis et al. (1982); Rose et al. (1994); Yao et al. (1994); and Zhang (1998)]. From these studies economic theory implies that pollution abatement policies reduce production and thus decrease national income.

There has been substantial debate about whether environmental policies do or do not influence domestic employment (Hopkins 1992). So far it is difficult to come to any precise conclusions, though at least in the short run, negative effects caused by a cutback in production will lead to a considerable decline in employment (Zhang 1998). However, in the long run, environmental policies will result in investment in pollution control equipment and thus create more employment opportunities. According to the OECD (1985), with few exceptions employment levels rise with pollution-control expenditure, particularly under some variants in the United States, France and, especially, Norway.

Denison (1979) and Crandall (1981) show that environmental regulations adopted in the 1970s have a negative effect on U.S. productivity growth. Investigations on five OECD countries reveal that productivity levels are usually lower than they would have been without environmental programs (OECD 1982). Many empirical studies show that, in general, the impact of environmental polices on industrial production costs is very small because pollution abatement costs constitute a very small portion of industrial costs on average, [Tobey (1990), OECD (1985), Smith and Ulph (1982), and Jaffe et al.(1995)].

Moreover, in some industries the implementation of environmental policies leads to positive productivity effects. It is argued that environmental policies induce "more cost-effective processes that both reduce emissions and the overall cost of doing business......" (U.S. Environmental Protection Agency 1992). Porter and Linde (1995) further point out that, from a dynamic view, environmental regulations provide incentives for technical innovation and hence in some industries productivity will rise in response to "properly crafted environmental regulations". The impact of environmental protection costs on product prices also has received attention [Pasurka (1984), Mutti and Richardson (1977), Walter (1973), Robinson (1988)].

Among the contributions to the impact of environmental policies on the balance of trade and payments, works by Baumol and Oates (1975) and Robinson (1988) are worth mentioning. Based on a two-final-good model, Baumol and Oates (1975) analyze the trade impacts of industrial pollution abatement costs and derive the balance of trade conditions for a two-good two-country world. According to this model, only direct abatement costs have an impact on prices and thus on the balance of trade and payments. Robinson (1988) measures the impact of marginal changes in industrial pollution abatement costs on the U.S. balance of trade in general, and on the balance of trade with Canada in particular. His work shows that environmental policy has a significant negative effect on the balance of trade, if environmental costs are fully reflected in commodity prices.

As is well known, free trade policy is designed to allow markets to allocate resources according to their most efficient uses, while environmental policy seeks to manage and maintain the earth's resources efficiently. Though conflicts may arise where the same resources are subject to both trade and environmental purposes, "on the most fundamental level, trade and environmental policy must meet in the concept of sustainable development. Both trade policy and environmental policy must serve that concept as their ultimate goal." (EPA Trade and Environment Committee 1991).

Hudson (1993) provides a useful starting point on the issues related to trade, environmental policy, and sustainable development. He argues that an environmental perspective on trade should not be construed as anti-trade, since trade can be an important instrument with which to achieve development that is economically and environmentally sustainable. He points out that in the long run environmental policy will not be successful if it ignores the development needs of the world's poor. On the other hand, the benefits of a more liberalizing trading system cannot be sustained over the long-term, if environmental and natural resources considerations are not taken into account. The impacts of trade liberalization and globalization on sustainable development have been examined by recent empirical case studies [Dragun and Tisdell (1999) and Jha, Markandya, and Vossenaar (1999)]. Those studies suggest that trade liberalization and globalization appear to have a negative impact on agricultural sustainability in developing countries. Thus in order to achieve sustainable development to reconcile trade and the environment is a key issue.

PATTERNS OF TRADE AND COMPARATIVE ADVANTAGE

Economic analysis would suggest that environmental policies raise production costs and hence encourage reduce specialization in the production of polluting outputs in countries with more stringent environmental regulations [Pethig (1976), Siebert (1977), McGuire (1982)]. In other words, countries with less stringent environmental policies could increase their comparative advantage in the production of environmentally sensitive goods. However, this standard trade theory is challenged by a more recent revisionist view. Porter and Linde (1995) argue that tight environmental policies are actually positive forces driving private firms and the economy as a whole to become more competitive in world markets by spurring innovation in environmental technologies. These conflicting views have since then led to a heated debate (Stewart, 1993). Tobey (1990, 1993) approaches this problem empirically by examining environmental policy and patterns of world trade. Following earlier studies on shifting patterns of international trade Leamer(1984), Bowen (1983), Brecher and Choudhri (1988), Murrell (1990), Trefler (1994), and Leamer and Levinsohn (1995) have also contributed. The Hecksher-Ohlin-Vanek (HOV) model is a multi-factor and multicommodity extension of the H-O model (Vanek 1968, Melvin 1968, and Leamer 1980). Tobey employs a cross-section HOV model to test the hypothesis that the stringency of environmental policies is directly related to the exports of pollution intensive commodities. Results indicate that there is no significant linear relationship between the stringency of environmental policy and the net exports of the pollution-intensive commodities. Thus environmental policy has no significant impact on patterns of world trade.

According to classical trade theory, a country's comparative advantage stems from differences in technologies and in factor endowments (as compared with the respective conditions of its trading partner). Since the 1970s numerous theoretical studies have tried to examine the impact of environmental policy on comparative advantage [Siebert (1977), Siebert et al (1980), Pethig (1976), McGuire (1982), Baumol and Oates (1988), Krutilla (1991), Carraro and Siniscalo (1992), Brander and Taylor (1997), and Markusen (1997)].

Siebert et al. (1980) have employed a two-commodity-two-country model to investigate possible different technologies as determinants of comparative advantage. They confirm that a country's technological comparative advantage to produce less pollution-intensive goods is strengthened by environmental policy. This group also examines comparative advantage generated from differences in relative factor abundance, which include divergences in the quality of resource endowments and in demand conditions. Their study treats a country's emission standards as a factor endowment. Using partial equilibrium analysis Baumol and Oates (1988) demonstrate that if a country does not impose environmental policy when the other country does, then the first country will increase its comparative advantage or decrease its comparative disadvantage in the pollution-intensive industry, and it will then specialize in that industry at the cost of environmental degradation. Brander and Taylor (1997) more recently investigate the question of whether countries with 'low standard' (LS) resource management policies might have a comparative advantage over countries with 'high standard' (HS) resource management policies. As mentioned before, Porter and Linde (1995) challenge the received view relating environmental policy and comparative advantage by arguing that comparative advantage does not depend on static efficiency or on optimizing within fixed constraints; rather it is a function of the capacity of a firm to initiate innovation and improvements in order to shift those constraints. Antweiler et al. (1998) suggest that trade changes the composition of national output in a more polluting way for capital– abundant countries. This implies that the developed countries have comparative advantage in producing pollution–intensive goods. On the contrary, Kalt (1989) finds that environmental regulations in the U.S. have led to a sharp reduction in net manufacturing exports in 1977 presumably due to a shift of output mix toward the production of clean air and water, and away from pollution- intensive outputs.

TERMS OF TRADE

According to trade theory, a change in terms of trade may increase or lower the social cost of attaining a given target of environmental quality. Therefore, it is worthwhile to examine whether a country will be able to share its costs of the imposition of environmental policies with the rest of the world *via* a terms-of-trade improvement. Siebert et al. (1980) investigate the analytical links between alternative levels of the emissions standards in a country and any possible resulting changes in terms of trade. By means of comparative statics, they show that free trade with direct pollution control in the form of an emissions standard policy enables the acting country to improve its terms of trade, if the production of the exportable good is relatively emissions intensive. According to Bhagwati (1971), a production tax is the most efficient solution to controlling production pollution, while a consumption tax is the optimal response to consumption pollution. Using this principle, Magee and Ford (1972) provide a fruitful analysis of the implications of alternative pollution abatement taxes for the terms of trade in the United States. Their results show that if a production tax is imposed on the export sector, export prices and the price of domestic goods will increase and hence the tax improves the U.S. terms of trade. Studies are lacking in explaining how pollution taxes influence the terms of trade of the developing countries.

Transnational pollution issues (for example, acid rain and the pollution of the Great Lakes or industrial pollution and the Rhine river) have inevitably become a serious problem for governments throughout the world. To solve this problem the countries involved should adopt some abatement strategies appropriate to control trans-border pollution. To examine the impact of these strategies on terms of trade, Merrifield (1988) constructs a two-country general equilibrium (GE) trade model with pollution and introduces two abatement strategies, production taxes and the abatement equipment standard. Merrifield employs the model to analyze the impact of abatement strategies in the context of the acid rain deposition problem between the U.S. and Canada. Merrifield shows that if the two countries jointly and simultaneously levy a production tax, production in both countries will not change and, consequently, the terms of trade will remain unaltered. Similarly, if both countries agree to raise their abatement equipment standards, there will be no change in the terms of trade if the elasticity of substitution of capital for labor is similar in the two countries. He also demonstrates that if Canada adopts a stricter abatement standard, the terms of trade will be shifted in Canada's favour. This work pays attention to the analysis of the effect of abatement strategies on transnational pollution.

PATTERNS OF PRODUCTION AND CONSUMPTION

Environmental protection policies may lead to sectoral structure distortion in the conservationist country. This distortion is reflected by changes in product prices and in sectoral production. Similarly, a reduction in emissions of certain pollutants may cause a change in sectoral production. Using a partial equilibrium input-output framework, Pasurka (1984) has analyzed the magnitude of the impact of environmental protection costs on U.S. product prices in 1977. This result shows that for most U.S. industry sectors, environmental protection costs do not result in significant price increases. By means of a CGE model, Zhang (1998) empirically investigates the impact of CO2 emission limits on China's sectoral production. According to Zhang, aggregate gross production tends to contract at an increasing rate as carbon dioxide emission targets become more stringent. The results indicate that, given reductions in CO2 emission, an economy will move toward labor-intensive sectors.

The literature on environmental supply impacts has been inconclusive. According to Leontief's (1970) input-output study, assuming that the elimination of pollution can be achieved by use of intermediate products from sectors other than anti-pollution and that final deliveries to households remain constant, the output of all the productive sectors clearly will increase. The OECD (1985) investigates the effects of various environmental programs on the levels of GDP in selected OECD countries.

There are also few studies that analyze how environmental policy influences consumption. Using macro econometric models, the OECD (1985) examines the impact of environmental protection programs on the aggregate demand components of some of its member countries.

LINKAGES BETWEEN TRADE, ENVIRONMENT AND THE ECONOMY

The basic objective of trade policy is to liberalize international trade and to attain the benefits of comparative advantage. These benefits help a country to specialize in the production of goods and services that it can produce more efficiently. Accompanying the process of specialization, however, environmental problems may crop up due to the externalities of specialization. In order to solve those problems governments often have to provide certain kinds of environmental regulations or incentives that to some extent either in conflict with trade policies or alter them significantly. The conflicting relationship between trade and environmental policies has received both an economic and a political focus since the 1990s [(Housman and Zealke (1992), Jackson (1992), and Saunders (1994)]. Audley (1997) points out that the conflicts between trade and environmental policy often involve the competitive differences between national and international environmental policies. The rise in non-tariff barriers reported by the WTO raised concern that environmental policy would become a new form of non-tariff protection (Runge 1990, 1993). Under the guise of environmental policies, foreign products might be prohibited from access to markets where domestic products are more expensive (Snape 1995, and Stokes 1992). In most cases, governments set standards and impose those standards on their trading partners, as part of their effort to set international standards for environmental protection. Due to the absence of an effective international enforcement mechanism, some countries have to resort to unilateral actions. Under most circumstances, unilateral actions are a violation of existing WTO jurisprudence (Bhagwati and Patrick 1990, and Durbin 1995). Housman and Zaelke (1992) discuss some options for reducing or eliminating the conflict between trade agreements and environmental policy. The main thrust of these options is to incorporate environmental considerations into trade agreements.

The recent interest in transnational pollution and trade involve two issues. First, does free trade increase transnational pollution? Second, is "green" trade policy an efficient way to regulate transnational pollution? Copeland and Taylor (1995b) examine the first issue using an approach different from earlier studies such as Merrifield (1988) and Rauscher (1991). They develop a multi-good, many-country trade model in a general equilibrium setting. The model is used to explore how welfare and pollution levels are affected by free trade in goods and pollution permits, by international income transfers, and by international agreements limiting or reducing pollution emissions respectively. The authors also demonstrate that in factor price equalized trade equilibrium, trade raises the level of pollution generated by each Southern country, lowers the pollution level generated by each Northern country, and leaves world pollution unaffected. The authors further investigate the effect of income on trade and world pollution and find that the pre-trade world income distribution determines how trade will affect the environment. If the world distribution of income is highly skewed, then free trade increases world pollution; but if countries have relatively similar incomes, then free trade has no adverse effect on pollution.

Literature on the efficiency of green trade policy by Baumol (1971), Markusen (1975), and Rauscher (1991) shows that it may be in one country's interest to use trade policy in order to reduce transnational pollution from abroad. Maestad (1998) goes further by arguing that the use of green trade policy may be desirable from a global point of view as well, because such measures may promote global economic efficiency. Based on the analysis of a two-country partial equilibrium model, the author concludes that when some countries are reluctant to internalize environmental costs, efficiency in the global economy may be enhanced by regulating the trade with these countries. This study also shows that the usefulness of green trade policy is not restricted to the transnational pollution case; trade provisions may promote global economic efficiency when some countries take unilateral steps towards solving local environmental problems as well.

There are many studies that evaluate the relations between natural resources and trade, [Withagen (1985), Puttock and Sabourin (1992), and Park and Labys (1999)]. The theoretical linkages between natural resources and international trade are many and varied. Studies attempt to integrate natural resources and international trade usually captures one or both of the two essential features of the asset nature of natural resources. These include the rate of change of the resource stock over time and /or the long-run equilibrium condition on the rate of return from holding the resource (Dasgupta et al. 1978).

Hazardous substances usually refer to those which have a direct or indirect negative impact on environmental quality (pesticide, chemicals, and hazardous wastes, for example). Since the 1980s, there is an increasing evidence of potential or actual damage due to exports of hazardous substances. Scherr (1987) and Azevedo (1982) survey the evolution of U.S. regulations of such trade. The main issues in the U.S. involve the listing of ingredients or chemical components of exports and imports, explicit bans on drugs which are domestically prohibited, and procedures for altering importing countries of the export of hazardous substances. Xing and Kolstad (1996) point out that pattern of waste trade include two routes. One route is from a high-income country to a low-income country. The other route is between industrialized countries where the waste flows are from a country with abundant assimilative capacity to the one that has scarce assimilative capacity.

In the past two decades, a large number of studies have addressed the issue of global warming and trade. However, there is no discussion about the role of trade in the global warming process. On the contrary, there are many studies on the trade effects of greenhouse gas (GHG) abatement and the use of trade measures to limit GHG emissions in order to slow down the global warming process. Whalley and Wigle (1991) quantitatively investigate the effect of GHG abatement on the terms of trade between fuels and final goods. They have explained that the terms of trade between fuels and final goods are potentially sensitive to GHG abatement. Burniaux et al. (1991a, b) and Symons et al. (1990) have conducted similar research. These studies also show that the terms of trade between fuels and other goods will be altered no matter how abatement is achieved, but the direction of change depends on whether the (explicit or implicit) carbon tax is collected and kept by consumers or by producers. The issue of how GHG abatement influences changes in international competitiveness has also received some attention, [Glomsrod et al. (1992) and Blitzer et al. (1990)]. Competitive issues arise if abatement falls unevenly across countries. Unfortunately, the greater the abatement, the higher are industrial costs and the less competitive the economy. In recent years, various forms of international GHG emissions trading systems have been studied (Manne and Richels, 1996, and Edmonds et al., 1997). It is believed that emissions trading can bring about substantial potential abatement cost savings compared with abatement measures such as international GHG taxation and quotas. Antweiler et al. (2001) set out a theory of how openness to international goods markets affects pollution concentrations. They develop a theoretical model to divide trade's impact on pollution into scale, technique and composition effects and then examine this theory using data on sulfur dioxide concentrations from the Global

Environment Monitoring Project. They found that international trade creates relatively small changes in pollution concentrations when it alters the composition, and hence the pollution intensity of national output. Their estimates of the associated technique and scale effects created by trade imply a net reduction in pollution from these sources. Combining their estimates of scale, composition and technique effects they conclude that free trade is good for the environment.

POLLUTION REDEPLOYMENT TO DEVELOPING COUNTRIES

The relationship between national environmental policy and capital mobility has been studied extensively since the 1970s, [Cumberland (1979) and (1981), McGuire (1982), Oates and Schwab (1988), Sinn (1994), Wellisch (1995), and Schneider and Wellisch (1997)]. In order to analyze the movement of capital across frontiers caused by environmental regulation, McGuire (1982) incorporates an environmental factor, in the form of effluent output, as an input of the polluting industry into a two-factor-and-two-country Heckscher-Ohlin model. If capital is freely mobile across boundaries, the least differential regulation between countries will entirely drive out the regulated industry from the more to the less regulated economy. An interesting discussion on environmental policy and capital mobility is presented by Schneider and Wellisch (1997). Given that production technologies are the same in both sectors and the elasticity of substitution between capital and labor is positive, they argue that in order to keep the outflow of the factor rewards to emissions low, the non-traded-good sector receives relatively more emissions permits. The traded-good sector experiences a capital inflow while the non-traded a capital outflow, and fewer non-tradables will be produced. This drives up the price for non-tradables. Hence the authors conclude that restricting the outflow of emissions rents results in relative generous pollution allowances in the non-traded-good sector.

Another concern relates less to environmental outcomes and more to environmental regulation. Most studies that trace the link between trade and the stringency of an environmental standard explore either the industrial flight (pollution–haven) or industrial specialization hypothesis. The “industry flight hypothesis” suggests that since the developed countries impose tougher environmental policies than do the developing countries, polluting industries shift operations from the developed to the developing countries; developing countries thus become “pollution havens.” It is argued that increased international competition for investment will cause countries to lower environmental regulations (or to retain poor ones), a “race to the bottom” in environmental standards as countries fight to attract foreign capital and keep domestic investment at home. (World Bank 2000) This hypothesis is analogous to tax havens which apply low rates in order to attract financial capital. It implies a deliberate strategy on the part of host governments to purposely “undervalue” the environment in order to attract new investment. (Jenkins et al. 2002). According to Xing and Kolstad (1996), this hypothesis is based on three arguments. First, environmental policies will increase the production costs of the polluting industries. Second, tough environmental policies discourage new investment away from the polluting industries. Third, since some policies directly confine the range of products or the inputs of production, producers have to relocate their production in other areas. Ulph and Valentini (1997) probe the issue using a model of two countries, two industries, an upstream and a downstream sector, and two firms in each industry. The authors come up with some surprising results. The effect of environmental policy imposed in one industry can sometimes be positive: i.e., a country imposing a small emissions tax can attract firms from other industries to locate in that country. Leonard and Duerksen (1980), Walter (1982), Pearson (1987), Leonard (1988), Lucas, Wheeler and Hettige (1992), Low and Yeates (1992), Friedman (1992) and Levinson (1996) empirically investigate the industry flight hypothesis. They found little or no evidence that environmental regulations have a significant impact on the investment and location decision of firms. Mani, Pargal and Huq (1997), Gray (1997), and Wheeler (2000) offer a counter–argument for this hypothesis. Levinson (1996) employed firm- level data on location choice and pollution abatement costs to assess the effect of state environmental regulations on new manufacturing plant locations in the U.S. Levinson indicates that the limited evidence of industry flight stems from firms that have plants in several states following the most stringent environmental regulations in all locations. Mani, Pargal and Huq's (1997) study of new plant locations in India indicate that environmental spending, presumably occurring as a result of more stringent regulation, is likely to be higher for more pollution- intensive industries. Gray (1997) notes that firms want to locate where the markets are and that polluted areas may have shrinking markets, hence driving some firms away. On the contrary, Lucas et al. (1990) and List and Co (1999) found some support for the industry-flight hypothesis. Lucas et al. suggest that implementation of progressively strict environmental regulations in the OECD countries have led to significant location displacement of pollution–intensive industries. List and Co (1999) study shows that regulatory expenditures per manufacturer and the location decision of new firms are inversely related in West Virginia.

There are several other approaches in this context which can also be explored. According to classical trade theory based on differences in factor endowments, the polluting industries (including such industries as chemical, ferrous and non-ferrous metals, pulp and paper, and oil refining) are more likely to conglomerate in capital-abundant developed countries, and to a lesser extent, in economies in transition and newly industrialized countries(WTO 1999). In East Asia in the 1970s, for example, the fast growing "Tigers" (Korea, Taiwan China, Singapore and Hong Kong) began to export more products of certain highly polluting sectors, while Japan began to reduce its exports in these sectors. However, this trend diminished in the 1980s, and a stable pattern emerged with the Tigers importing somewhat more than they export in the highly-polluting sectors. In China the share of the five dirtiest industries in total industrial output has fallen, while imports of pollution intensive products have actually increased (World Bank, 2000). A similar pattern occurred in trade of pollution intensive products between North America and Latin America (World Bank 2000). For the US, there appears to be evidence for the hypothesis that stringency of environmental regulation is a source of comparative disadvantage in dirty industries (Mulatu et al. 2004). Smarzynska and Wei (2004) found some support for the "pollution haven" hypothesis, but the overall evidence is relatively weak and does not survive numerous robustness checks. Wheeler (2000) provides examples of the link between air pollution regulation and FDI in Mexico, Brazil, India, and the U.S. that illustrate the importance of community, or firm level efforts, to internalize the costs of pollution in developing countries.

Leonard and Duerksen (1980) analyze trade and investment data to find whether the differences in environmental control costs have led to industrial flight toward developing countries. Their study shows that, instead of developing countries, the receivers of most foreign investment in polluting industries such as paper, chemicals, metals and petroleum refining are other industrial countries. Moreover, the percent of U.S. foreign direct investment in polluting industries in developing countries compared to developed countries did not show a significant increase over time. Hence they conclude that there is no evidence of the flight of U.S. industries to developing countries. Based on his study on the trend in foreign direct investment by firms from Western Europe, Japan, and the United States in the 1970s, Walter (1982) reaches the same conclusion. Although there exists a large amount of overseas production in polluting industries, there is little evidence that it has been caused by differing pollution abatement costs and that foreign direct investment is fleeing to countries with less stringent environmental policies. Pearson's (1987) survey also supports the conclusion that there is little evidence of industrial flight to developing countries. According to Leonard (1988), the industrial flight and pollution haven hypotheses are not convincing because they are based on too static and too narrow a definition of comparative advantage. Again, the author finds no supportive evidence for the industrial flight and the pollution haven hypotheses. However, gains obtained from lenient environmental policies were not great enough to change the locational preferences of multinationals since other considerations such as labor supply, infrastructure and political stability appeared much more important in location selections. Lucas, Wheeler, and Hettige (1992) econometrically test the hypothesis that environmental policies drive polluting industries from the OECD countries to developing countries. The estimates show that economic growth has a significantly smaller effect on toxic emissions in open economies than in closed economies. If the industrial flight hypothesis held, then developing countries with open economies would have experienced a rapid growth of toxic emissions density. Their investigation finds that this is not the case in reality. Low and Yeats (1992) support the industrial flight hypothesis. The authors conclude that stringent environmental policies in developed countries probably lead to the shift of polluting industries from developed to developing countries. Xu (1999)'s study on bilateral trade found no evidence that a country with stricter environmental standards lowering their total exports of pollution–intensive goods. According to OECD (1997), most pollution-intensive FDI originating in industrialized countries were going to other developed countries, rather than to developing ones. Even in the developing countries, the amount of inward investment in pollution-intensive industries was a smaller proportion of total FDI receipts in 1992 than in 1972. To support the same argument, Letchumanan and Kodama (2000) support the hypothesis finding no evidence between FDI flows and pollution content of an industry for developing countries. According to their findings, Singapore and Thailand have negative correlation indicating that FDI is occurring in relatively clean industries, whereas overall the United States and Germany have higher correlation with pollution intensive industries compared to the developing countries. Moreover, investments into the U.S. are occurring in more polluting industries than investments from the U.S. to the rest of the world. They have also mentioned that investments into Germany, as compared to outward investments, are occurring in cleaner industries and outward investments from Japan are realized in less pollution intensive industries. On the contrary, Co *et al.* (2003) have investigated the United States FDI into developed and developing countries through two manufacturing industries. Using annual panel data on US direct investment into several countries from 1982 to 1992, and constructing two-step selection model, they confirm that environmental regulations are influencing the U.S. Among others, Bartik (1988), Levinson

(1996) and List (2001) argue that environmental standards and FDI flows are inversely related for the average developing country. This negative relation, however, may not be the case for all developing countries.

Furthermore, Kolstad and Xing (1998) attempt to evaluate empirically the effects of the stringency of environmental policy on the location of the polluting industries, and declared that the stringency of environmental regulations did matter in the case where other determinants of FDI remained constant. There exists statistically significant negative linear relationship between FDI of the U.S. chemical industry and the stringency of environmental policy in a foreign host country. In general, according to their study, lax environmental policy tends to attract FDI from U.S. pollution intensive industries. Smarzynska and Wei (2004) have found some support for the "pollution haven" hypothesis by using firm-level data set describing investment decision by 534 major multinational firms in 24 countries from Central/Eastern Europe and the former Soviet Republics instead of country/industry level. The major supportive evidence arises when a country's environmental standard is measured by its participation in international environmental treaties. A recent study shows FDI originating from Hong Kong, Macao and Taiwan is attracted to provinces with a relative abundance of low-skilled labor, and relatively weak environmental controls. In contrast, FDI from non- Chinese sources is attracted by high levels of skilled labor and by high pollution levies—the reverse of the pollution haven hypothesis (Dean et al. 2004). Copeland and Taylor (2003) analyse theoretically and examine empirically the validity of Pollution Haven Hypothesis and Factor Endowment Hypothesis using data on measured sulphur dioxide concentrations from over 100 cities worldwide during the period 1971 to 1986. The results suggest that free trade will shift pollution-intensive goods production from poor countries with lax regulation to rich countries with tight regulation, thereby lowering world pollution.

Eskeland and Harrison (2003) find almost no evidence that investors in developing countries are fleeing environmental costs at home. Using data from four developing countries (Cote d'Ivoire, Mexico, Morocco, and Venezuela), they examine the pattern of foreign investment with an analysis of U.S. outbound investment between 1982 and 1994. They reject the hypothesis that the pattern of U.S. foreign investment is skewed toward industries in which the cost of pollution abatement is high. On the other hand, Waldkirch and Gopinath (2004) have found evidence of a pollution haven effect from Mexico albeit limited to only a few industries. Other than that, FDI is largely driven by Mexico's comparative advantage in labor-intensive production processes. For other pollutants that are less regulated or come largely from non-industry sources, no systematic relationship between FDI and pollution is detected. Busse (2004) finds no evidence to support the pollution-haven hypothesis that industries facing above-average abatement costs with environmental regulations would relocate their activities in pollution havens. The exception is iron and steel products, where a negative and statistically significant link is established, implying that higher compliance with international treaties and conventions and more stringent regulations are associated with reduced net exports.

Thus literatures on environmental regulations-FDI linkage have shown that few studies achieving robust and meaningful empirical evidence support the theoretical background while others are not robust or at least far from giving a complete support to the analytical framework. Hence, meticulous studies need to be performed in this field.

ENVIRONMENTAL DEGRADATION

The close linkages between trade and the global environment have been widely recognized yet remain heavily disputable [Baumol (1971), Grossman and Krueger (1993), World Bank (1992), French (1993), Bhagwati (1993a), Daly (1993a), Chichilnisky (1994), Copelead and Taylor (1994), (1997), and (1999), Perroni and Wigle (1994), Lopez (1994), and Selden and Song (1994)]. In cases such as the shipment of low-cost tropical timber from Malaysia to Japan, and the U.S. exportation of lead car batteries to a plant near Sao Paulo, one could infer that trade affects the global environment negatively. However, in many other cases, world trade has demonstrated positive environmental effects as well. For example, fuel-efficient Japanese cars not only reduce air emissions in the United States but also force U.S. manufacturers to develop more fuel-efficient models. French (1993) summarizes that trade and trade-induced integration of the world economy is shaping global environmental trends in several ways. First, trade intensifies the environmental impacts of domestic production by expanding international markets. Second, trade makes it possible for countries to obtain from other countries the desired products that are domestically either unavailable or protected by strict laws Third, since national environmental policies and even some international environmental treaties are often treated as "non-tariff barriers to trade", efforts to restore environmental quality within countries and to protect the global commons, such as the atmosphere and the oceans, are erroneously misjudged. In the debate over the environmental consequences of free trade, Bhagwati (1993a) argues with Daly (1993a) that environmentalists are wrong to fear the effects of free trade. In responding to the widespread fear among environmentalists that free trade accelerates economic growth and that growth harms the environment, Bhagwati points out that the fear is misplaced since growth enables governments to tax and to raise resources for objectives such as pollution abatement and the general protection of the environment. For instance, rich countries today show greater concern about the environment than do poor countries. In addition, an empirical study by Grossman and Krueger (1993) also shows that some environmental quality indicators improve as income increases. Therefore, in Bhagwati's opinion, international trade should generally help protect the environment, rather than harm it. On the other side of the debate, Daly (1993a) contends that the free traders seek to maximize profits and production without taking into consideration social and environmental costs. In this case environmental costs would rise faster than would any production benefits and the economy would enter an anti-economic phase that impoverished rather than enriched itself. Chichilnisky (1994) addresses the trade and the global environment issue in a different way. She thinks that the problem reflects a North-South dimension. Developing countries in the South tend to over-produce and export environmentally intensive goods even if they are not well endowed with them. Developed countries in the North, on the other hand, tend to over-consume, even if trade equalizes all traded goods and all factor prices worldwide. She also examines some environmental policies and shows that taxing the use environmental resources in the South is not always reliable since it can lead to more over-extraction if the resources are exploited using labor from a subsistence sector. The author suggests that property-rights policies may be more effective for improving environmental and trade linkages.

In response to Bhagwati's (1993b) argument that trade promotes economic growth and that growth improves environmental quality, Daly (1993b) proposes that trade can induce environmental degradation and that degradation can lead to income losses and these income losses can result in further environmental degradation. Copeland and Taylor (1997, 1999) examine the environmental consequences of trade. If there is no trade, the productivity of the environmentally sensitive industry will be harmed by the production of the polluting manufacturing industry. With trade exists, the two incompatible industries can move away from each other. Hence, trade can help to reduce cross-industry production externalities and to improve global productivity gains. Lopez (1994) investigates the economic growth, trade, and environmental degradation relationship in a different setting in which unilateral trade liberalization in a small open developing economy is focused on. The results of the analysis show that the stock effects of environmental resources on production are closely related to the impacts of economic growth and trade liberalization on the environment. The World Bank (1992) concludes that international trade as such cannot be regarded as a cause of environmental degradation, but what causes this degradation is the absence of appropriate environmental protection policies. It is emphasized that trade could improve the allocative efficiency of environmental goods among and within countries and hence reverse environmental degradation. Lucus, Wheeler and Hettige (1992) focus their empirical study on air pollution and economic growth using data from both developing and developed countries over 1960-1988. The authors find that air pollution, in general, does not decline with economic growth. Specifically, the income effect on pollution intensity tends to be negative in more open countries while it is positive in closed economies. This study implies that even though trade may not improve the environment, it at least does no harm to the environment. Perroni and Wigle (1994) show that compared to environmental policies, trade policies have little impact on environment quality. Though liberalised trade may more or less deteriorate the environment, its relative contribution to environmental degradation is quite insignificant.

FACTOR REWARDS

The costs incurred by environmental policies can be passed forward to the consumers of the polluting products, and/ or backward to their factors of production. It seems, however, that the issue of how environmental policies affect factor rewards has not yet received much attention in literature. Moreover, studies on the issue have been theoretical and general equilibrium in nature, [Yohe (1979), Siebert *et al.* (1980), McGuire (1982), and Merrifield (1988)]. Another common feature of these studies is the use of a two commodity and two-sector framework in which one sector is polluting and the other nonpolluting. Yohe (1979) examines the incidence of stricter pollution standards on labor and capital rewards, given the assumption of fixed output prices in both sectors. Yohe concludes that real returns to capital and labor move in opposite directions and that the shadow price of pollution increases when environmental policies become more restrictive. If the non-polluting sector is labor (capital) intensive, the transfer of production factors from the polluting to the non-polluting sector leads to a higher capital labor ratio and an increase (decrease) in labor reward, and at the same time a decrease (increase) in capital reward. Siebert *et al.* (1980) investigate the case where both sectors produce homogenous emissions. Their study shows that if one sector is strongly pollution intensive, while the other is strongly capital (labor) intensive, then tighter pollution standard results in a rise (decline) in the capital reward and a decline (rise) in the labor reward. If neither of the sectors is relatively pollution intensive, a tighter standard reduces the rewards of both factors. McGuire (1982) introduces international trade and emissions damages, and assumes a fixed marginal social cost of pollution. He concludes that environmental regulation results in movements of capital and labor rewards in opposite directions and the rewards of capital and labor depend on the elasticity of demand for the polluting good and on the relative capital/labor intensity of the polluting good in comparison with the non-polluting good. The author concludes that, for a small country with no influence over world commodity prices, pollution control regulation decreases the reward of the factor used intensively in the production of the polluting sector and raises the reward of the other factor. For a large country, its uncoordinated regulation will increase the world price of the regulated commodity, and the reward of the factor used intensively in the production of the regulated commodity will increase worldwide. Merrifield's (1988) analysis reveals that a production tax will cause changes in factor rewards. Specifically, if a country's exporting commodity is taxed, the consumer's price rises and the producer's price falls, and both capital and labor rewards decrease in that country. If a restrictive abatement equipment standard is adopted in either country, the relative scarcity of products in the adoptive country may increase. The scarcity will be reduced if the country can absorb the excess capital supply released from the reduction in pollution. Therefore, once the production of pollution control equipment is capital intensive enough, the excess capital supply will lower the rewards for capital and raise the rewards for labor in both countries.

According to the Heckscher-Ohlin theory, resource endowment is the key factor leading to trade. However, the conventional Heckscher-Ohlin model usually includes only two resource factors of production, namely labor and capital. Some economists now recognize that other resources such as the environment, as well as other productive resources such as land and other natural resources, should be taken into consideration for more realistic models and theories, [Abbott and Haley (1988), Lopez (1994), McGuire (1982), Merrifield (1988), and Yohe (1979)]. Environment as a resource has been incorporated into the Heckscher-Ohlin model as a factor of production by Yohe (1979), McGuire (1982), and Merrifield (1988). Lopez (1994) uses a different neoclassical general equilibrium set up but the treatment of the environmental resource is about the same. The environmental factor is usually measured in those analyses in physical quantity of emissions to the environment as a result of production. The relationship between environmental policies and the prices of this factor revealed in those studies is rather straightforward. In the case of no environmental policy, firms can discharge whatever amount of effluent generated in production into the environment without any costs. Thus, the price of the environmental factor is virtually zero. In general, the stricter an environmental policy, the higher the marginal abatement costs and hence is the higher the price of the environmental factor. There is little evidence on how environmental policies affect the rewards to land and other natural resources such as energy and materials when treated as factors of production.

Since the present study is addressing trade and the environment issue using input-output methodology, next section is briefing the literature on this.

TRADE AND ENVIRONMENT USING INPUT-OUTPUT MODEL

Since the 1970s, the use of the international I-O model helps one explain relationships between one country's imports and another's exports and the reciprocating effects of trade via both quantity flows and price levels, [Petri (1976), Torii *et al.* (1989), and van der Linden et al. (1995)].

Moreover, the feedback effects of various international trade policies such as tariff reductions and trade liberalization can be conveniently simulated and analyzed [Torii et al. (1989) and Almon *et al.* (1991)].

Bulmer-Thomas (1982) demonstrates that I-O models can be used to the investigation of comparative advantage and patterns of international trade in an economic development context. The rationality of patterns of trade is examined using the relative factor content of exports and imports (the ratio of capital to labor content of exports and imports). Extending I-O models to include interactions between the environment and the economy began in the late 1960s, [Ayres and Kneese (1969), Leontief (1970, 1973), and Leontief and Ford (1972), Forsund (1985) and Forssell and Polenske (1998)]. Since the 1970s, as a result of increasing concerns over global warming and other transboundary pollution problems such acid deposition, environmental I-O models have evolved to give special emphasis on energy production and consumption (Leontief *et al.* 1977, and Ireland 1993, among others). As a response to the challenge of *Limits to Growth* (Meadows et al 1972), Leontief et al. (1977) modeled energy and environmental policy within a detailed global I-O framework. The world economy is divided into fifteen regions. A fixed coefficient I-O model with 45 sectors and including resource requirements, in particular, energy requirements, and emission abatement activities is built for each region. All separate regional I-O models are linked through international trade. An important conclusion of the study is that the availability of energy as well as other resources and requirements for environmental protection do not act as obstacle to the economic growth of developing countries. Ierland (1993) employs a non-linear dynamic I-O model to analyze economic, energy, and environmental policy in an open economy of the Netherlands from 1950 to 2010 (1950-1988 for parameter estimation and 1990-2010 for policy scenarios). The impacts of environmental policy differ substantially among branches of industries due to the fact that the intensities of energy, labor, capital, and pollution, and that the import and export coefficients are not the same for any of the branches, the economy is further disaggregated into separate sectors such that the environmental and energy characteristics of the branches show up clearly. In addition, the model not only includes the most important economic variables for the various branches of industries, it also computes the demand for energy in physical units for different fuel types and for the branches of industries, transportation, households and government. This model provides a useful tool for both the "hypothetical" policy makers and the "actual" policy makers to obtain an overview of the impact of different sets of policy measures such as an increase in volume of international trade and a reduction in the level of household taxation, and the impact of the changes in external circumstances such as environmental strategies adopted in foreign countries. Clearly, the model can also be used as a framework for trade and environment interaction analysis.

It should be noted that many applied and computable general equilibrium (AGE, CGE) models are used to study economic, trade and environmental analysis and thus extended I-O models by explicitly incorporating a supply and demand system. In those CGE or AGE models, parameters of the behavioral and structural equations are either calibrated to data of certain single year or estimated econometrically, [Jorgenson and Wilcoxen (1993) and (1990), Hazilla and Kopp (1990), and Whalley (1991)].

Several other attempts also have been made on trade environment issue by considering input-output model (Wright, 1974; Wyckoff and Roop, 1994; Gale and Lewis, 1995; Antweiler, 1996; Lange, 1998; Proops et al., 1999;

Lenzen and Mungsgaard, 2002; Machado et al., 2001; Munksgaard and Pedersen, 2001; Wadeskog, 2002). The cross country studies in this respect are by Gerilla et al. (2002) for China and Japan, Przybylinski (2002) for Poland and Germany, Hayami and Nakamura (2002) for Japan and Canada and Ahmed (2002) for selected OECD countries. But only a few have addressed the PHH and FEH using I-O model (Mukhopadhyay 2004; Mukhopadhyay & Chakraborty, 2005 a, b).

Gale and Lewis (1995) also extend I-O applications to include trade liberalization and environmental pollution issues. The authors have developed a detailed I-O model of production and trade in the Mexican economy, where CO2 emissions are measured by fuel use in production and trade consumption, while free trade-induced change in production and trade is expressed by a change in total emissions. Based on this model, the authors first determine the changes in production and trade that result from the implementation of NAFTA. Then these results are used to estimate the change in the quantity of CO2 emissions for each industry. The results suggest that free trade with North America increases Mexico's total CO2 emissions but it also shifts resources away from more pollutive to less pollutive sectors.

Though goods and services traded in a globally interdependent world, the consumption in each region is linked to green house gas emissions in other regions. Although the green house gas responsibility of the inhabitants of a region is determined by their consumption of domestically produced goods or imported commodities international negotiations on emission reductions focussed solely on national emissions, i.e. emissions arising from the respective country. Thus, greenhouse gases embodied in international trade are neglected. Recently, Munksgaard and Pedersen (2001) have highlighted this point. They have demonstrated in their work that the

Danish greenhouse gas balance is dependent on whether producer or consumer responsibility is assumed. It has been argued that in order to get equitable reduction targets, international trade has to be taken into account when assessing national responsibilities for abating climate change.

Most studies dealing with energy and greenhouse gases in a closed and open input-output model employ single region models. These single region studies are based on the assumptions that commodities imported from foreign countries are produced using domestic production technology and energy inputs. However, this assumption is not necessarily valid. Recently, Lenzen and Munksgaard (2002) have made an extension of the existing single region model as described by Munksgaard and Pedersen (2001) and Lenzen (2001) by introducing a multi regional input-output model to calculate the amount of energy and green house gases embodied in a value unit of commodities produced for Danish final consumption.

Some specialists have been particularly concerned with the impacts that international trade might have on the effectiveness of climate change agreements. Among them work of Wyckoff and Roop (1994) can be mentioned. In this article global warming policies based on reducing domestic greenhouse gas emissions ignore the carbon embodied in international trade flows, which could be important if emission reduction schemes include only a subset of emitting countries. This analysis shows and discusses implications of the finding that a significant amount (about 13%) of the total carbon emissions of the six largest OECD countries is embodied in manufactured levels of export and import and eco efficiencies (pollution or natural resource requirements per money unit of product). Machado et al. (2001) applied I-O techniques to the Brazilian economy to evaluate the total impacts of international trade on its energy use and CO_2 emissions.

Results show that in 1995 in Brazil carbon embodied in the exports of non-energy goods are larger than the relevant amounts embodied in the imports of non-energy goods. Haan (2002) has derived environmental balance of trade by analysing the trade relationships for a number of trade patterns of the Netherlands. These bilateral environmental balances of trade are further analyzed by tracking down differences in the absolute levels of export and import and eco efficiencies (pollution or natural resource requirements per money unit of product). Lange and Hassan (2002) have shown that the structure of exports of Botswana, Namibia and South Africa is heavily weighted by water intensive products based on agriculture, forestry and related activities and mining, as in many developing countries. Since water is a scarce resource in these countries they have assessed using a CGE model the introduction of the user pays principle for water pricing in South Africa and Botswana.

The work of Gerilla *et al.* (2002) has studied the transfer of technology between China and Japan and its effects on the embodied carbon emissions generated from the transfer based on the inter-country I-O table of Japan and China for 1985 and 1994. The results show that increased emission of embodied carbon has occurred due to the transfer of technology. Przybylinski (2002) has analyzed the bilateral flow of trade between Poland and Germany to find out their effects on environment in both countries. Full effects are measured using I-O tables. The paper aims at constructing the balance of pollution flows between these two countries for 1995, considering main types of air pollutants. Recently Hayami and Nakamura(2002) have linked the I-O table of Japan and Canada using trade data and estimated CO_2 emission through bilateral trade between each sector(405 sectors in Japan and 479 sectors in Canada).They have found significant difference of CO_2 emission per production between these countries. The paper suggests the reallocation of alternative technologies to reduce CO_2 emission between these two countries. Ahmed (2002) investigates how important international carbon flows are for a number of OECD countries. The paper uses the OECD input-output and SSIS databases, together with assumptions on the amount of carbon embodied in different energy sources, to estimate the total amount of energy and carbon embodied in the imports of manufactured goods and services in each country.

The review of the literature suggests that the empirical evidence is still far from clear (Copeland & Taylor, 2004). The methodologies employed to test the hypotheses are widely varied so are the results Discussions on Thailand's trade-environmental relation received attention in recent years (World Bank 1994; UNCTAD/UNDP, 1994; UN, 1995, Pantumvanit, 1995; TDRI 1996, 2000; Jha *et al.*,1999; TEI 2000; APFEED 2002 and Li, 2005). Pantumvanit (1994) explores the relationship between trade and the environmental consequences through four case studies focused on legislation and agreements resulting from the US marine and Mammal protection act, the Montréal protocol, the international tropical timber agreement and the international standards organization 14000 series of environmental standards. Jha et al. (1999) have shown in their book how changing trade regimes have affected the environment and how stricter environmental regulations have affected trade. The book has given particular importance to developing and transition countries where the relationship between trade and the environment has a major impact. Thailand has also been undertaken in their study. This study was based on few important sectors like fishing, textile, agriculture, timber and electronics and concluded that Thailand has become more intertwined with other countries, but also more dependent on them. Certain measures imposed by importing countries, including those for environmental purposes, may limit the market access of Thai producers for specific products. Li (2005) explores the question of whether there is a trade-off between trade liberalization and environmental quality in Thailand using a computable general equilibrium framework. The author examines the economic, environmental, and welfare impacts of alternative policy scenarios, including a tariff reduction scenario, a carbon tax scenario, and a combined trade and environmental reform scenario. The results of the analysis show that if the country were to pursue greater trade liberalization alone without a concomitant increase in pollution abatement, there is a modest but real risk that it will become more specialized in dirty activity. If the country pursued pollution abatement without further trade liberalization, the cost in terms of growth does not appear to be significant. When environmental and trade policies are jointly considered, greater substitution away from the polluting energy inputs is observed with the cost on economic growth remaining insignificant. Some works capture sector specific performance (Patmasiriwat D, Kuik O and Pednekar S, 1999). Thailand is the world's leading exporter and the largest producer of Black Tiger prawns, and supplies 20 percent of the world trade in shrimp and prawn. Intensive shrimp farming causes negative environmental and socio-economic impacts. Marine shrimp farming has encroached upon about 17 percent of Thailand's mangrove forest area and environmental pollutants such as nitrogen, phosphorus, suspended solids, chemical and drugs, and antibiotic substances, not only pollute off-site environments, but they also cause on-site pollution, threatening the long-term sustainability of the sector.

Unfortunately no comprehensive work has been done on Thailand involving issues discussed above in particular using I-O techniques. Do environmental regulations influence trade patterns as predicted by the pollution haven hypothesis (PHH) in Thailand? Is Thailand's trade influenced by factor endowment hypothesis (FEH)? Is there any implication of FDI on the environment? So the current book will be addressing these issues.

3

The Structure of Thailand Economy

The present day Thailand has a long historical past. The origin of the Thai people can be traced to southern China around 1000 years ago. After coming to present day Thailand, they formed the Sukathai Kingdom around 1238, following a rebellion against the ruling Khmers. In 1350 the kingdom was moved to Ayutthaya. In 1767 Burmese invaders completely destroyed Ayutthaya. The kingdom was reunified under King Taksin, a survivor of the rout. He established his base in 1768 at Thonburi along the western side of the Chao Praya River. In 1782 the capital was moved to Bangkok on the opposite bank by king Budha Yodhfa (Rama1 1782-1809), who was the first king in the Chakri dynasty, which progressively extended the rule of Siam-south along the Malaya peninsula, north to Laos and east into Cambodia (Paitoonpong & Abe, 2004).

Since then there has been a varied change in Thailand passing through ups and downs in social, political and economic life. The economic development process of any society involves a large number of social, political, administrative and external factors, both in terms of causes and consequences. Thailand is no exception. To give a full account of these factors in case of Thailand is difficult in this chapter. What will be attempted here is to focus in brief on the salient features of Thailand's economic development in last two decades.

GROWTH OF THE ECONOMY

Among all south and south East Asian countries Thailand can be regarded as one of the fastest growing economy. Until recent years, economic development in Thailand was considered a success story, not only because of the nation's rapid growth and structural changes, but also because of the development strategy, which relied on market mechanism conducive to trade and investment. Despite ups and downs, the Thai economy appeared to grow well with reasonable stability for over three decades. From 1960 to 1996, annual economic growth in Thailand averaged nearly 8.0 per cent. During the decade from 1986 to 1996, Thailand was one of the fastest growing economies in the world, with annual growth soared at an average annual rate of 9.5 per cent. And it reached a historic record of 13.3% in 1988. Figure 3.1 shows Thailand's GDP trend from 1980s till 2004. The curve shows a rising trend throughout except a downfall in 1998 due to financial crisis. The Thai economy experienced negative GDP for two consecutive years, i.e, -1.4 per cent in 1997 and –10.8 per cent in 1998. Figure 3.2 shows the degree of responsiveness of Thailand's GDP growth with the factors like agriculture and non-agriculture. It reveals that Thailand's GDP growth is much influenced by the nonagricultural growth which was led by the buoyant expansion in the manufacturing sector (Figure 3.2). The detail year wise performance of the same is given in Table 3.1.

AGRICULTURAL SECTOR

In any economy the role of the agricultural sector cannot be minimized. So is also in the case of Thailand. In 1960,

Table 3.1
Growth rate of Thailand's GDP, Agriculture and Non Agriculture

	1980	*1981*	*1982*	*1983*	*1984*	*1985*	*1986*	*1987*	*1988*
GDP at constant 1988 price (billion baht)	913.7	967.7	1,019.5	1,076.4	1,138.4	1,191.3	1,257.2	1,376.8	1,559.8
GDP (% change)	4.6	5.9	5.4	5.6	5.8	4.6	5.5	9.5	13.3
Agriculture (% change)	0.8	5.1	2.5	4.8	4.4	4.5	0.4	0.1	10.5
Non-agriculture(% change)	5.6	6.1	6.1	5.8	6.1	4.7	6.8	11.6	13.8
	1989	*1990*	*1991*	*1992*	*1993*	*1994*	*1995*	*1996*	*1997*
GDP at constant 1988 price (billion baht)	1,750.0	1,945.4	2,111.9	2,282.6	2,470.9	2,693.0	2,941.7	3,115.3	3,072.6
GDP (% change)	12.2	11.2	8.6	8.1	8.3	9.0	9.2	5.9	-1.4
Agriculture (% change)	9.6	-4.7	7.3	4.8	-2.4	5.0	4.0	4.4	-0.7
Non-agriculture(% change)	12.7	14.1	8.8	8.6	9.8	9.5	9.8	6.1	-1.4
	1998	*1999*	*2000*	*2001*	*2002*	*2003*	*2004*	*2005*	
GDP at constant 1988 price (billion baht)	2,749.7	2,872.0	3,008.4	3,073.6	3,237.6	3,460.0	3,671.7	3842	
GDP (% change)	-10.5	4.4	4.8	2.2	5.3	6.9	6.1	4.5	
Agriculture (% change)	-1.5	2.3	7.2	3.2	1.0	8.7	-4.8	-2.4	
Non-agriculture(% change)	-11.4	4.7	4.5	2.0	5.8	6.7	7.4	5.2	

Source: Bank of Thailand, Thailand's Key Economic Indicators.

Figure 3.1: Thailand: GDP at Constant Price, 1980-2004

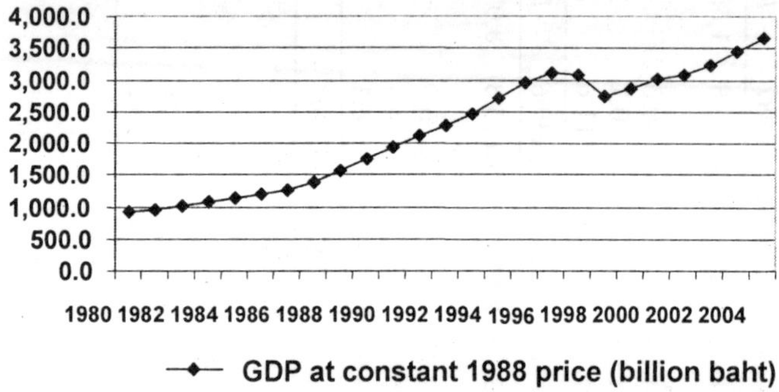

Figure 3.2: Agriculture and Non Agriculture (% change)

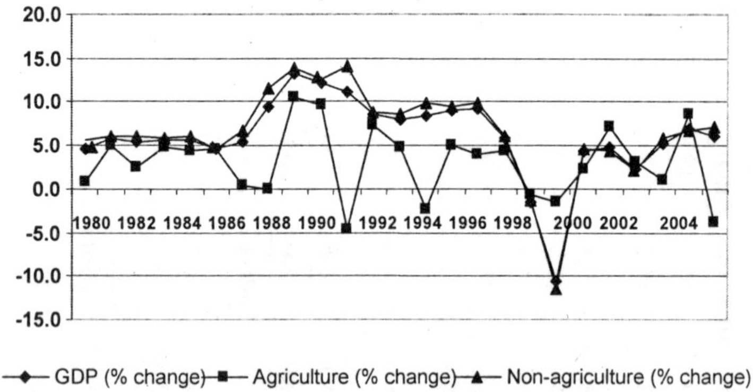

the agricultural sector accounted for over 40 per cent of the country's GDP and 80 per cent of its exports. With the passage of time its importance gradually declined. In early 2000, the share of agriculture in the GDP is about 10 per cent. Agricultural growth has been possible due to its favourable climatic condition combined with the favourable crop prices and the impact of government's agricultural price support measures. These measures induced farmers to expand planted acreage. This accounted for the sharp increase in crop production almost by 10-11% during 1980s to 1990s. Notable increases were observed for rice, maize, and rubber. Crop substitution programs led to gains in such secondary crops as millet, beans and kenaf. Sugarcane and tapioca observed considerable growth in spite of some crop damages due to intermittent rainfalls and floods. But in 1990 the agricultural growth slowed. It registered a negative growth. Unfavourable climatic conditions, including drought at the beginning of the planning season, a severe flood before the harvesting season, and an outbreak of pestilence are responsible for the negative growth. Output of major agricultural crops declined. Rice output fell, while output of maize and sugarcane also declined despite favourable prices. Output of cassava declined which performed well in the 1980s. During the period 1980s to 1990s, other branches of agriculture enjoyed growth including animal husbandry. Livestock production continued to increase. Fishery and forestry sectors performed well throughout. Fishery catch rose considerably as a result of increased fishing activities outside Thailand's territorial waters which were made possible by relaxed restrictions of neighbouring countries and by successful joint fishing ventures with other countries (Bank of Thailand, Annual Report). In addition coastal fish farming also expanded rapidly, especially of black tiger prawns. However, the fish catch came down slightly in the 1990s as fishing outside territorial water expanded only marginally while fishing within the territories suffered from the damage to marine resources caused by the typhoons at the end of 1989, in addition to the domestic price increase for high speed diesel gasoline. Forestry production started falling from 1989 following continued forest closure. After the 1990s farmers have been hit by the increasing cost of imported inputs such as fertilizers and seeds, while farm price declines. It creates a massive shuffle in the Thai agricultural production. Major crops output slowed down from the mid to late 1990s particularly output of rice, which was induced by the fall in price of rice and the reduction in plantation area. The output of cassava and sugarcane also declined due to the insect infestation. Despite the price fall in rice, the average price of major crops rose on average by 3.2%. This resulted in an increase in farm income of 5.4% which helped to raise farmer's purchasing power which, in turn, boosted domestic consumption. This sector's contribution contracted by 4.4 per cent and registered negative growth for four consecutive quarters of 2004 with a significant decline in livestock as a result of the bird flu in the first half and latter half of the year. The fishery growth declined in line with the production of shrimp export. The crop was also affected by drought in the last quarter of 2004.

On the whole Thailand's share of agriculture in GDP has declined from more than 30 per cent in the 1970s to about 9 per cent in 2004. This long-term decline reflects in part the slow growth of demand for farm products compared to the faster growth in demand for manufactured goods and services due to rising incomes. It also reflects supply side factors, especially capital accumulation, which resulted in resources moving out of labor intensive agricultural industries and into more capital- and skill-intensive manufacturing and services industries. In addition, Thai economic policy has contributed to the long-term decline in agriculture. Although expenditures by Government are high by regional standards, public investment in agricultural research and investment has been modest. Private capital investment in agriculture, especially in crop production, is also rather limited. In addition, trade policies have encouraged the development of capital intensive manufacturing, giving that sector an edge when competing for domestic resources. As a result, yield improvements in Thai agriculture are among the lowest in the region. While agricultural production did not grow as rapidly as output in other sectors during the economic boom, neither did it contract as in other sectors during the economic crisis. The policy debate on agriculture sector development has increased sharply since the emergence of the economic crisis. The sector not only absorbed large numbers of the urban unemployed, but also became an important source of increased foreign exchange earnings without the need for large capital inputs.

PERFORMANCE OF THE NON AGRICULTURE SECTOR

From an economy dominated by agriculture, Thailand shifted steadily toward industrialization. Non-agricultural sectors have grown rapidly, capturing increasing shares in the country's GDP (Table 3.1 and Figure 3.2). It includes mainly manufacturing sectors and services. The expansion of the industrial sector in the sixties was helped by a number of favorable factors, including abundant supplies of natural resources and labour, and economic and political stability (Bank of Thailand, Annual Reports). The government's policy of promoting industrialization through private enterprise and massive investment in infrastructure in this decade also contributed to industrial growth. It grew by 10.7% during the 1980s with the manufacturing, construction, trade and services sectors experiencing particularly high growth rates.

Manufacturing sector output, intended for foreign as well as domestic market, expanded 12.6% annually in the late 1980s and the early 1990s (before the crisis of 1997). The rapid growth was due to higher incomes, greater purchasing powers, and favourable condition in domestic and foreign markets, while production costs remained low (Bank of Thailand, Annual Reports). Export oriented industries which expanded significantly included textiles, canned food, plastic products, rubber products, footwear, ceramic products and computer components. Industries producing primarily for the domestic consumption also exhibited an upward trend. Vehicles transport components, construction material, beverages, household electrical goods, and small diesel engines for agriculture registered high growth rates (more than15 %). Expansion in the textiles, automobiles, transportation equipment, gunny bag industry, beverages and manufacture of air conditioning units and construction materials continued to be rapid. The noticeable growth can be observed in case of construction sector at the rate of 11% annually despite rising prices of construction materials and continued shortages. Mining and quarrying expanded satisfactorily, particularly the activities related to industrial minerals (13% growth rate). Its output also rose due to the increased production of the quarrying industry to support the construction boom combined with an expansion in the production of petroleum products, including natural gas for electricity generation and crude oil. In the services sector, tourism industries continued to expand markedly as a result of public –private cooperation in promotional activities coupled with the strong yen and European currencies. Thailand remained an interesting and inexpensive destination for tourists.

Since the onset of the economic crisis in 1997, capacity utilization in the manufacturing sector has decreased significantly. Manufacturing sector showed a slight positive growth of 1.6 per cent in 1997, but turned sharply negative to –11.4 per cent in 1998. In 1998, the Bank of Thailand calculated the rate of capacity utilization by industrial enterprises at around 52.8 per cent, compared to over 70 per cent before the crisis. Many industries including food processing, beverages, iron and steel, and transport equipment were still operating at less than 50 per cent of their production capacity. Among all manufacturing industry transport sector dominates. But domestic sales of motor vehicles dropped drastically after the crisis. In 1998, production in most industries in the manufacturing sector has shown major declines. The average capacity utilization in this industry dropped to

23.4 per cent in 1998, with passenger cars registering a very low rate of 13 per cent. From 1999, capacity utilization in the manufacturing sector has picked up, but many industrial sectors still suffer from low production capacity. Recovery followed with 11.5 per cent growth in 1999 and 5.9 per cent in 2000. However, since the second half of 2000, the momentum of the manufacturing sector has slowed markedly. In 2001 the economy including the manufacturing sector lost ground. During the first three quarters of 2001, the manufacturing sector grew only by 1.3 per cent, although it picked up slightly to 1.5 per cent in the last quarter. The general conditions in manufacturing remained weak till 2001. The average rate of capacity utilization in 2001 was 53.7 per cent. Only a few industries have shown noteworthy improvement in their production indices after 2000. These include transport equipment, vehicle tires, block rubber, jewelry, and beer. Construction materials have also shown signs of picking up in 2001 as a result of recovery in the construction sector. Manufacturing sector showed some recovery with an estimated growth rate of 5.4 per cent in the first half of 2002. It enjoyed the benefit of growing domestic and external demand. In 2003 it grew by 10.3 per cent and continued to contribute the most to the economic growth. In response to the higher demand, the industrial production and capacity utilization increased. In 2003 the utilization rate averaged at 66.2 per cent. Industries that have already utilized full capacity are, for example, the upstream petrochemical, zinc metal, galvanized iron sheet, integrated circuit, and hot- and cold-rolled sheet (NESDB, 2004). In 2004 it expanded by 8.3 per cent at the slower rate as last year's growth of 10.4 per cent because food production slowed down whereas other manufacturing goods continued to expand. The slowdown in the food production was partly due to the reduction in sugar production (because of the restriction in sugar-cane cultivated areas and drought) and frozen poultry production. For production of vehicles and equipments, commercial car production increased whereas commercial car production grew at a slower rate. Financial, construction, telecommunication, transportation, and tourism sectors have also expanded rapidly (NESDB, 2005).

INDUSTRIAL POLICY IN THAILAND

Since the Second World War, the Thai government has placed great importance on industrial development. The Ministry of Industry was established in 1942 to encourage and monitor development in this sector, with other government agencies participating directly or indirectly in the formulation of industrial policy. These include, for example, the formulation of development strategies by the National Economic and Social Development Board (NESDB), tax policies by the Ministry of Finance (MOF), investment promotion by the Board of Investment (BOI) and trade policies on agricultural and industrial products by the Ministry of Commerce (MOC).

Industrial development policies in Thailand have changed over time. After the war, a number of state enterprises producing a variety of products were set up to promote industrialization. However, since the late 1950s, policymakers began to place more emphasis on private enterprises. In the First Social Economic Development Plan (1961-1966), it was stated that the government would reduce its involvement in manufacturing. The public sector would focus on providing private companies with investment incentives and constructing vital infrastructure needed for industrial development. In 1959, the Board of Investment (BOI) was set up to provide tax breaks and other incentives to private investors. Tariff structures were revised several times in the 1960s and 1970s to give more protection to domestic industries.

The industrialization strategies of the 1960s emphasized production for the domestic market. Import-substitution industries including assembly activities using largely imported parts and components were promoted. Foreign direct investment (FDI) was enthusiastically encouraged. The import-substitution strategy helped to make a quick start on industrialization. Many foreign producers and assemblers of consumer goods came to invest in Thailand.

The import substitution strategy was later criticized for failing to produce significant linkages among industries and relying heavily on imported inputs. In the early 1970s, when industrial growth slowed down and the country's balance of payments turned to deficit after many years of surplus, the government started to adopt export promotion strategies. The promotion of manufactured exports was mentioned in Third Economic and Social Development Plan (1972-1976). In 1972 the investment promotion law was revised to give more incentives to export industries. Starting from a small base, manufactured exports have expanded rapidly since then.

The export promotion strategy has continued until recently. But the country's industrial structure has also been diversified toward intermediate and capital goods industries. Since the late 1980s there have been increasing investments in intermediate products, including parts and components for computers, automobiles, and electronics.

Along with export promotion, the policy on dispersing industrial activities to different regions in the country was mentioned in the third plan. The revision of investment promotion law in 1972 also enabled the BOI to provide more incentives to business firms operating in designated provincial areas. In the same year, the Industrial Estate Authority of Thailand (IEAT) was established as a state enterprise under the Ministry of Industry (MOI) to promote the creation of industrial estates in different regions of the country.

An important element in Thailand's industrial development during the 1980s was the development of the eastern seaboard as a major alternative industrial zone. The Fifth Plan's Eastern Seaboard Development Programme was set up during the fifth-plan period after the discovery of natural gas in the Gulf of Thailand. A gas separation plant was built. Infrastructure, including highways, deep seaports, and industrial estates was constructed. Petrochemical and steel plants were set up in the Mab Taput industrial estate in Rayong. Light and export industries were located in the Laem Chabang industrial estate in Chonburi along the eastern seaboard.

In the fifth development plan, a structural adjustment programme was formulated with a view to promote labor-intensive, resource-based and export-oriented industries, and gradually phasing out inefficient operations through rationalization of incentive structures. Promotion of small, medium-sized and rural enterprises was also included. Industrial policy planners began to realize some of the problems resulting from rapid industrial expansion, for example, chronic trade deficits due to heavy reliance on imported components and parts, and the emergence of inefficient industries protected by high tariffs. However, due to the unfavorable economic conditions during the fifth-plan period, the structural adjustment programme was not implemented.

The sixth development plan (1987-1991) continued to give priority to export, small scale and regional enterprises. Agro-based and "engineering" industries such as metal, machinery, electronics and communication equipment were also included. The promotion of regional industries was again emphasized in the seventh plan (1992-1996). This time the policy was supported by more concrete measures. A committee on regional development was set up, and differential incentives were offered to industries located in different areas of the country.

During the sixth and seventh plan period (1987-1996), there were increasing foreign investment projects in intermediate and machinery-related industries, particularly for the production of electronic and automotive parts and components. The country's industrial structure has since then become more diversified with greater numbers of intermediate and capital goods enterprises. The export structure of the county has also changed. Computer parts and electronic and electrical products have become important export items for Thailand.

Industrial Policy Liberalization in 1993

In the early phase of industrialization various protective measures were employed to protect domestic infant industries from domestic and foreign competition. This continued period of protection had adversely affected the economy producing an inefficient allocation of the country's resources due to the lack of incentive for producers to improve production efficiency as well as reducing competition and thus detrimental to the interests of consumers.

In order to promote a more efficient allocation of resources and to achieve a more competitive environment in the industrial sector, the authorities have relaxed protective measures covering various important industries. The relaxation started with the permission to establish new plants or to expand existing capacity of some industries in a given period and eventually abolishing restrictions on the to reduce the monopoly power, to encourage competition thereby boosting production efficiency in industries which were formerly represented by only a few producers. This helps enhance the competitiveness of Thai industries against foreign competitors in terms of improvements in the product quality and production costs. During the past five years, protective measures have been reduced in various industries. For example, new entries are freely allowed in several industries, namely steel bars, cement, glass sheet, yarn, fabrics, diesel engineers, downstream petrochemical products and small-scale factories.

Liberalisation in the Manufacturing Sector in 1995

The authorities continued to deregulate the manufacturing sector to allow domestic industries to adjust and prepare for competition under global trade liberalization.

The Ministry of Industry issued a long-term policy on the petrochemical industry as follows: Permitting free establishment and expansion of petrochemical plants of all types; expansion of raw material producing plant for intra-industry use and floating the trading prices of petrochemicals, both raw materials and finished products.

Strengthening National Energy Security

The National Energy Committee approved the long-term plan for the development of power generating capacity by ECAT (1995-2011) which aims to strengthen the security of the country's energy system. The plan comprises "the master plan" governing investment for expansion of production and transmission systems.

Several policies considered being important in the previous plans, including promotion of export industries, small-scale and regional industries continued to be emphasized in the eighth development plan (1997-2001). There were also more concerns for environmental protection, industrial standards, technological capabilities, productivity improvement and protection of intellectual property rights. "Supporting industries" including parts and components and packaging, etc. were also specified as industries to be promoted.

During the eighth plan, the Thai economy plunged into the worst recession of the post-war period. The country suffered a sharp economic downturn in1997 and 1998 with a combination of currency and financial crises. The economic crisis was the cumulative effect of a number of structural weaknesses. Among the structural weaknesses were the loss of competitiveness of Thai products in world markets, and the failure of institutions in both the corporate and government sectors to adapt to rapid changes in the era of globalization.

Industrial Liberalisation in 1997 abolished the prohibition of establishing or expanding the production of engines and motorcycles. In addition, the local content requirements for motorcycle production were also lifted.

Industrial Measures in 1998 established various industry development institutes as proposed by the Ministry of Industry to enhance potentials and efficiency in the development of domestic industries in the long term. Establishment of various Automobile Institute and Electricity and Electronics Institute was encouraged. In addition National Research and Development Institute for Precious Stones and ornaments was set up during that period.

An Industrial Restructuring Programme (IRP), aimed at improving the long-term capabilities of 13 broad industrial sectors, was initiated in 1998 to address limitations in technology, manpower, marketing, and management, as well as problems resulting from industrial growth such as pollution and over-crowded urban areas. The IRP is implemented by the Ministry of Industry (MOI), although it receives support from other government agencies as well. The programme was designed to improve the long-term competitiveness of the country's 13 major industrial sectors: food processing, textiles and garments; leather products and footwear; wood products and furniture; pharmaceutical and chemical products; rubber, plastic, ceramic, electronic and electrical products; motor vehicles; gems and jewelry; iron and steel; and petrochemical products. These industries comprise the bulk of industrial products in Thailand. The objectives of the IRP include upgrading of industrial technology, development of more sophisticated product lines, training, and more equitable distribution of production and employment opportunities across the country. But due to its modest scope and continuing weak conditions of the economy, the impact of the IRP has been limited.

For Industrial Protection the Ministry of Industry postponed the abolition of local content requirements for domestic vehicle parts for an unspecified period. Nevertheless, such requirements are automatically abolished by 1 January 2000 according to Thailand's agreement with the World Trade Organisation (WTO). In this regard, the Ministry of Finance expedites restructuring tariffs on imported inputs of the automobile industry as a whole before then.

At present, the ninth economic plan (2002-2006) is under implementation. The objectives specified in the plan are promotion of economic stability and sustainability; establishment of a strong national development foundation; establishment of good governance at all levels of the Thai society; and reduction of poverty and empowerment of the people to cope with changes. In industrial development, enhancement of competitiveness is emphasized. Among the major elements under this heading are restructuring of different production and trade sectors; upgrading the quality of infrastructure; improvement of productivity through the development of net work in different industrial sectors, and linking agencies in public and private sectors; development of small and medium enterprises; cooperation with neighboring countries; improvement of trade negotiation system; and promoting of science and technology and manpower development.

A review of industrialization policies in different national development plans helps to see the evolution of industrial policies in different periods. However, Thailand's official economic and social development plans are more indicative than mandatory plans. These plans present only broad policy guidelines, not detailed operational measures. In many instances, the policies sketched out a development plan fail to receive concrete support from government agencies. Furthermore, Thailand is as open economy greatly influenced by world events and constantly readjusting with global trends. Frequent changes of government also keep administrative officials focused more on immediate problems than on long term issues such as the competitiveness of the nation's industrial sector, and the overall development of science, technology and manpower. The articulation and implementation of coherent, long-term industrial development policy remains an important issue for Thailand.

THE STRUCTURE OF FOREIGN TRADE

Thailand has changed markedly over the last four decades. The economy has become more open over the years. International trade has expanded and foreign direct investment (FDI) inflows increased significantly. In the sixties, agricultural products accounted for the bulk of the country's exports. Manufactures were mostly directed to meet the domestic demand, and exports were modest. In the 1960s, the growth of the economy was led by considerable public-sector investments in infrastructure and by expanding private investment in manufacturing, especially in import-substituting industries. Although domestic markets remain significant, the manufacturing sector has clearly become more export oriented. Since the seventies, manufactured exports account for more than 80 per cent of the nation's total export value. With the continuing increase in fuel prices, worldwide inflation, and the decline of primary product prices in the world market since 1975, the terms of trade has become less favourable. However, there was a significant improvement in 1992/ 1993 with the sharp rise in primary commodity prices in the world market (UNIDO, 2002)

With increasingly large trade deficits (Table 3.2), Thailand decided to devalue its currency in 1981 and 1984.

Declining economic growth, sharp increases in global interest rates and currency devaluation led to widespread failures of finance companies. Contrary to expectation, however, a dramatic turnaround in economic conditions emerged in the second half of the eighties. From 1986 until the outbreak of the economic crisis in 1997, economic growth accelerated. Exports expanded, foreign-exchange receipts from tourism soared. Large inflows of foreign investment, and other forms of capital helped generate substantial surpluses in the country's balance of payments. In the late eighties, as a result of their currency appreciation, Japan and some newly industrialized economies (NIEs) relocated a number of their industries of Thailand. There were large FDI inflows in export-oriented and machinery-related industries during this period. Domestic investment in manufacturing, real estate and the stock market also saw unprecedented expansion. The average export-output ratio in the manufacturing sector has risen over time. Industries with high export ratio are canned food, milled rice and tapioca, sugar and other food products, textiles, wearing apparel, footwear, wood products and furniture, rubber products, electronic products, and electrical appliances (UNIDO, 2002).

As external trade expands more rapidly than domestic production, the Thai economy has become more open, with the proportion of exports and imports to GDP increasing significantly over time. Table 3.3 shows that in 2000, commodity exports and imports accounted for 55.68 and 51.25 per cent of GDP respectively. And the degree of

Table 3.2
External Account of Thailand

External Account (billions of US$)	*1980*	*1981*	*1982*	*1983*	*1984*	*1985*	*1986*	*1987*	*1988*
Export	6.4	6.9	6.8	6.3	7.3	7.1	8.8	11.6	15.9
(% change)	23.07	7.81	-1.44	-7.35	15.87	-2.73	23.94	31.81	37.06
Import	9.3	9.9	8.4	10.2	10.2	9.3	9.4	13.3	19.8
(% change)	24	6.45	-15.15	21.42	0	-8.82	1.075	41.48	48.87
Trade balance	-2.83	-3.02	-1.57	-3.87	-2.9	-2.2	-0.5	-1.6	-3.9
Current account balance	-2.07	-2.57	-1.04	-2.9	-2.1	-1.5	0.3	-0.3	-1.5
(% of GDP)	-6.39	-7.37	-2.84	-7.24	-5.02	-3.85	0.69	-0.59	-2.43
Net capital movement	2.5	2.5	1.7	1.5	2.5	1.9	-0.4	1.1	3.7
Balance of payments	0.26	0.08	0.14	-0.79	0.4	0.5	0.4	0.9	2.5
External Account (billions of US$)	*1989*	*1990*	*1991*	*1992*	*1993*	*1994*	*1995*	*1996*	*1997*
Export	19.9	22.9	28.3	32.2	36.6	44.7	55.7	54.7	56.7
(% change)	25.15	15.07	23.58	13.78	13.4	22.13	24.8	-1.9	3.8
Import	25.2	32.7	37.8	40.1	45.1	53.4	70.4	70.8	61.3
(% change)	27.27	29.76	15.59	6.08	12.3	18.40	31.9	0.56	-13.4181
Trade balance	-5.3	-9.8	-9.5	-7.9	-8.5	-8.7	-14.7	-16.1	-4.6
Current account balance	-2.4	-7.1	-7.4	-6.1	-6.1	-7.8	-13.2	-14.3	-3.1
(% of GDP)	-3.32	-8.32	-7.53	-5.47	-4.87	-5.39	-7.85	-7.9	-2
Net capital movement	5.7	9.7	11.3	8.1	10.5	12.2	21.9	19.5	-4.3
Balance of payments	4	3.8	4.2	3	3.9	4.2	7.2	2.2	-10.6

Contd....

External Account (billions of US$)	*1998*	*1999*	*2000*	*2001*	*2002*	*2003*	*2004*	*2005(1st quarter)*
Export	52.87	56.8	67.9	63.1	66.1	78.1	96.1	80.8
(% change)	-6.75	7.43	19.5	-7.1	4.8	18.2	23	16.5
Import	40.7	47.5	62.4	60.6	63.4	74.3	94.4	89.1
(% change)	-33.76	16.9	31.3	-3	4.6	17.4	27	28.7
Trade balance	12.2	9.3	5.5	2.5	2.7	3.8	1.7	-8.3
Current account balance	14.3	12.5	9.3	6.2	7	8	7.1	-5.1
(% of GDP)	12.7	10.2	7.6	5.4	5.5	5.6	4.3	....
Net capital movement	-9.8	-7.9	-10.3	-4.6	-4.2	-8	0.7	4.1
Balance of payments	1.7	4.6	-1.6	1.3	4.2	0.1	5.7	2.9

Source: Customs Department, Thailand.

Figure 3.3: Export and Import Performance of Thailand, 1980-2004

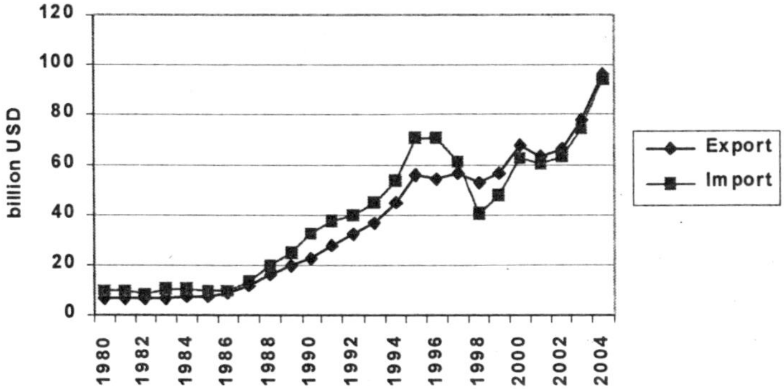

openness of the Thai economy in terms of foreign trade is thus 106.93 per cent in 2000 and rose to 123.2 in 2003.

Table 3.3
Percentage of Commodity Exports and Imports in GDP and Degree of Openness

Year	*Export/GDP*	*Import/GDP*	*Degree of openness*
1980	19.93	28.68	48.62
1981	19.76	28.41	48.16
1982	18.68	22.97	41.65
1983	15.75	25.44	41.19
1984	17.56	24.52	42.09
1985	18.15	23.98	42.13
1986	20.23	21.69	41.92
1987	22.93	26.3	49.24
1988	25.59	31.98	57.58
1989	27.46	34.86	62.32
1990	26.71	38.39	65.1
1991	28.75	38.61	67.36
1992	28.8	36.05	64.85
1993	29.11	36.11	65.23
1994	30.81	37.05	67.86
1995	33.01	41.93	74.94
1996	29.9	38.96	68.87

Contd....

Year	*Export / GDP*	*Import / GDP*	*Degree of openness*
1997	37.82	39.61	77.43
1998	47.14	36.27	83.41
1999	46.42	38.86	85.28
2000	55.68	51.25	106.93
2001	55.05	52.58	107.9
2002	65.90	53.51	123.2

Source: UNIDO, 2002.
[Here openness is defined as (export + import/GDP)]

Manufactures are now among Thailand's principal exports. Table 3.4 explains the sectoral export figures. Since 1998 exports of motor vehicles and parts have become the nation's principal export items. Major car assemblers have, in recent years, tried to increase their capacity utilization through exports. As a result of this rapid expansion, Thailand's share in world trade has gradually increased (Table 3.5).

Table 3.4
Sector wise Export Growth (percentage)

Sector	*1990*	*1995*	*1996*	*1997*	*1998*	*1999*	*2000*
Agriculture	16.96	11.4	11.84	10.18	9.39	8.35	7.1
Fisheries	5.51	5.06	4.5	4	3.97	3.56	3.31
Forestry	0.13	0.06	0.07	0.07	0.06	0.11	0.12
Mining	1.26	0.54	0.74	0.92	0.8	0.63	1.13
Manufacturing	74.67	81.87	81.54	82.42	82.3	84.27	85.53
Others	1.48	1.07	1.32	2.41	3.48	3.08	2.81
Total	100	100	100	100	100	100	100
	2001	2002	2003	2004			
Agriculture	7.34	7.62	8.35	8.36			
Fisheries	3.11	2.45	2.22	1.87			
Forestry	0.15	0.07	0.05	0.05			
Mining	0.91	1.04	1.15	1.29			
Manufacturing	84.93	85.72	85.92	86.78			
Others	3.56	3.11	2.32	1.66			
Total	100	100.00	100.00	100.00			

Bank of Thailand, Export Classified by Product Group.

Table 3.5
Share of Thailand's Exports in World Trade, 1970-2003

Year	*World Exports (thousand million USD)*	*Thailand's Exports (thousand million USD)*	*Share (%)*
1970	290.6	0.71	0.24
1980	1,945,90	6.51	0.33
1990	3,438,60	23.07	0.67
1991	3,530,90	24.43	0.69
1992	3,757,90	32.47	0.86
1993	3,765,80	36.97	0.98
1994	4,281,40	45.26	1.06
1995	5,120,20	56.44	1.1
1996	5,339,50	55.72	1.04
1997	5,229,00	57.37	1.04
1998	5,440,90	54.46	1
1999	5,623,70	58.44	1.04
2000	6,310,10	69.06	1.09
2003	707051	78.42	1.11

Source: IMF, International Financial Statistics, various issues.

DIRECTION OF THAI TRADE

Thai exports have mostly been directed to developed countries. The United States, the European Union (EU) and Japan were the three most important markets until the early nineties when sales to ASEAN markets surpassed the EU and Japan. In the last decade, shipments to the United States have increased significantly, with the US eventually taking about one-fifth of the country's total exports. Altogether, these four markets account for about 70 per cent of the country's total exports. In ASEAN, Thailand's single largest market is Singapore. The United Kingdom, the Netherlands, and Germany are the principal EU markets. Other important destinations for Thai products include China and the newly industrializing economies of Asia (Hong Kong,

Taiwan and South Korea), as well as Australia, Nigeria, Saudi Arabia and the United Arab Emirates.

Thailand's major export markets during the 1980s were the United States and Japan which together accounted for 36 per cent of total exports (Figure 3.4). The United States remained always the most important single market of Thai exports. The share of exports to Japan bears a rising trend followed by the EU while ASEAN's share dropped significantly. Indeed, Thai exports became increasingly diversified to newer trading partners such as Taiwan, the Republic of Korea, and Canada. The drop in ASEAN's share in 1988 was mainly due to the lower import shares of Malaysia and Brunei. But in case of imports in late 80s Japan and the United States, together accounted for 41.9% of the total import value. Imports from the Middle East rose sharply by 46% as a result of high growth rates of crude oil imports from Saudi Arabia, Kuwait and Iran. Meanwhile, the share of imports from the Middle East and the other countries raised considerably particularly those from Taiwan, the Republic of Korea, Hong Kong, and also Australia and Canada.

Figure 3.4: Direction of Foreign Trade of Thailand

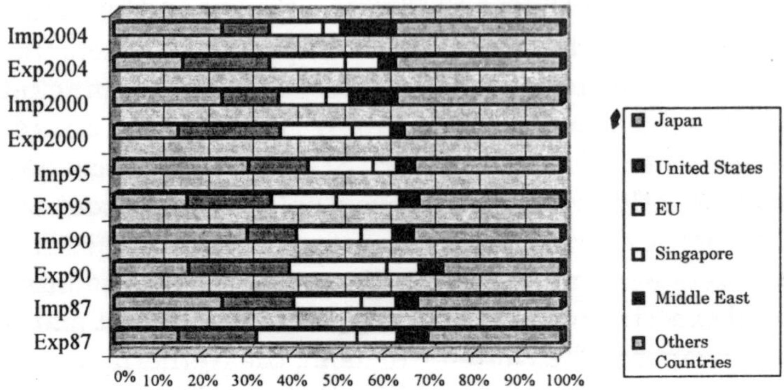

Thai manufactures rely heavily on imported materials. Products serving primarily the domestic market such as breweries and dairy products, animal and vegetable oil, animal feed, tobacco, pharmaceuticals, iron, steel and metal products rely much on imported materials. Some exports depend even more on imported components. Computer parts, integrated circuits, electricaland electronic products, and transport equipment are among the leading export items with high import content (Table 3.6).

Table 3.6
Import Content of Leading Exports from Thailand (%)

Commodity	*Import content*
Computer	64
Garment	44
Integrated circuit board	72
Rice	5
Rubber	3.5
Precious stones and Jewelry	46
Canned sea food	40
Shrimp, fresh and frozen	5
Radio, television and parts	40
Foot wear and Parts	40
Sugar	7
Vehicle, parts and accessories	53
Air Conditioning and parts	53
Fabrics	40
Plastic products	56
Rubber products	60
Plastic resin	57
Electrical adapter and parts	60
Tapioca products	10
Video and audio products	40

Source: UNIDO, 2002.

In fact, if the import of capital equipment used in the production of manufacturing goods is included, the manufacturing sector as a whole was a net user of foreign exchange. An export-oriented strategy, which is overly reliant on industrialization based on increasing volumes of imported inputs, equipment and technology, is likely sooner or later to impose serous pressure on the balance of payments (UNIDO, 2002).

After about a decade of import substitution in the 1960s, Thailand embarked on export industrialization in the 1970s. Both import-substituting industries and export industries expanded at rapid pace. The growth of the manufacturing sector until the mid-1960s was fueled by increasing domestic demand, robust exports, and rapid inflows of FDI. Manufactured exports from Thailand expanded at rapid rates during the 1970s and 1980s. It was observed that the export boom in the 1980s was made possible by new investment rather than by improvement in productivity (Warr, 1999). Also Thailand's industrial growth was accompanied by increasing trade deficits as industrial production in the country has been highly import dependent. Over time, there seems to be a deepening of industrial structure towards intermediate and capital products. The export structure of the country has also changed towards more sophisticated industrial products such as computer parts and electronic component. But these products are produced by foreign-owned companies using mostly imported technology. Thus, Thailand's industrial development has relied on imported technology and the technological capability of the indigenous has not been strong.

FINANCIAL LIBERALIZATION

Thailand's trade is greatly influenced by the financial sector. During the early nineties, greater demand for financial resources by domestic investors, together with the global trend on liberalization, led the Thai government to liberalize the country's financial system. In 1990, the Thai government officially accepted Article 8 of the IMF Articles of Agreement to liberalization of capital-movement took place. In 1993, the Bangkok International Banking Facility (BIBF) was established, allowing more financial institutions to set up operations in the financial system, and paving the way for Bangkok to become a regional financial centre (Wibulsawadi and Vongthieres 1994). Along with the liberalization of foreign-exchange controls other financial liberalization measures were allowing financial institutions to expand their scope of operations. The financial liberalization led to massive capital inflows, and helped the Thai economy to achieve high economic growth.

A significant proportion of the capital inflows were short-term loans as interest rates in the domestic market were much higher than foreign interest rates. There was also increasing investment in real estate and the stock market.

Since the mid-nineties, the real estate and property market has been saturated. This has hurt the financial sector as non-performing loans (NPLs) started to pile up. Share prices began dropping. Coupled with adverse conditions in the country's international account, these conditions led to a loss of confidence in the Thai economy, particularly in the country's financial sector.

The financial crisis in 1997 affected the real sectors of the Thai economy. Decreasing investment and the collapse of many companies led to sharp reductions in domestic expenditures and mounting unemployment. In 1997 and 1998, there were significant capital outflows and severe constraints on credit. The rigorous fiscal and monetary measures prescribed by the IMF and the foreclosure of many finance companies pushed the economy into deeper recession.

The baht was depreciated in 1984 even after the adoption of the managed-float system. The immediate effect of the depreciation was a significant increase in the burdens of companies with large foreign debts, including most financial institutions, and a number of large manufacturers. The cost of imported commodities rose sharply. The currency depreciation was supposed to benefit the country's export sector, earning more baht for exporters and rendering their products more price-competitive. However, the baht depreciation triggered a series of similar devaluations in the currencies of many other countries in the region. Furthermore, major importers of Thai products in Asia, including Japan and the ASEAN countries, were also suffering from economic slowdown. Demand for Thai exports was weak. Thus, the advantages gained by the depreciation of the currency were not impressive. Domestically, exporters faced a liquidity crunch following the crash. Thai industrial products in general have high import contents. The weaker baht increases costs for import dependent industries. In terms of US dollars, the value of exports decreased by 6.8 per cent in 1998. But imports were also greatly reduced. Thailand registered a trade surplus after the 1997 crisis.

After 1998, there were net capital outflows as massive amounts of capital left the country. However, there was a surge in FDI in the midst of the 1997 and 1998 crises. In 1998, there were large FDI inflows in the financial and retail trade sectors. In the manufacturing sector, some foreign investors injected capital into their affiliates, acquiring more shares in Thai companies. There were also new FDI inflows such as those in the automobile industry. However, after the surge in 1997 and 1998, net FDI in Thailand shows a declining trend. The last few years, Thailand experienced a sharp rise of the FDI from Singapore, driven by its high public sector savings and an outward looking strategy. According to the Bank of Thailand, Singapore was the biggest source of FDI in 2002, at $1.186 billion, followed by Japan at $660 million. U.S. firms accounted for $298 million in FDI in 2002, while the European Union (EU) accounted for an outflow of $451 million. Most investment from Singapore concentrated in finance, petroleum and real estate in the form of loans to affiliated companies. This contrasts sharply with Japanese investment, which focuses in share holding in manufacturing companies. The dominant industrial sectors capturing FDI in 2004 are machinery & transport equipment, electrical appliances and services. Among countries Japan and Singapore are the major investors in this respect.

SOCIAL IMPACT OF INDUSTRIALIZATION

An estimated 60 per cent of Thailand's population of 62 million people lives in rural areas, and 90 per cent of this number is farmer (NESDB, 2005). Nonetheless, rural households derive only 35 per cent of income from farming; the balance is attributable to non-farm activities and remittances from relatives who work in urban areas and overseas. An estimated 17 per cent of rural inhabitants live below the poverty line. The agriculture sector contributed about 10 per cent of total GDP in 1999, decreasing from about 20 per cent in the mid-1980s. The agriculture sector cushioned the social impact of the economic crisis by allowing re-migration from urban areas for an estimated 1.2 million people. Land and natural resources, already stressed before the crisis, have given way to increased environmental pressures (e.g., accelerated deforestation, soil degradation, and desertification). Improving productivity, enhancing export competitiveness, and improving sector management are the three key challenges facing the agriculture sector.

The rapid pace of industrialization in Thailand over the last four decades has had many consequences for the Thai economy. Among other things, it has resulted in higher income per capita and higher standards of living. Over the years, the structure of production and trade has shown a significant shift towards the industrial sector, as the growth rates of the industrial sector have been higher than that of the agricultural sector. The structure of employment has also changed as workers in the rural areas move to work in industrial and services activities in urban areas.

As a result of economic growth, per capita income of the Thai people has steadily increased over the years. Per capita income had increased from 2,100 baht in 1961 to 76,057 baht in 1997. The number of people living in poverty has also been reduced. Various studies have shown that the incidence of poverty has declined steadily over time. Different definitions of poverty lines present different figures, but all show a significant reduction of the percentage of people living under the poverty line as time passes. Comparisons of poverty incidence over time showed a decline from 30 per cent in 1975/76 to 21.2 per cent in 1988 (Tinakorn, 1992). More recent estimates made by the NESDB indicates that poverty incidence declined from 26.6 per cent in 1988 to 18.5 per cent in 1990, but increased slightly to 18.8 per cent in 1992 (Ratanalangkorn and Padungcheevit, 1995). Recently, the NESDB has constructed new poverty lines based on food requirements and non-food consumption of households and individuals. According to these estimates, 32.6 per cent of Thailand's population was identified as being poor in 1988. This figure was drastically reduced to 11.4 per cent in 1996. The economic crisis in 1997-1998, however, reversed this favorable trend, and the percentage of people living under poverty increased to 12.9 per cent, with 7.9 million people living under poverty in 1998 (NESDB 1998). A report released by the World Bank in May 2002 (World Bank, 2002) estimated that the poverty incidence was 14.2 per cent in 2000, and there were 8.9 million people living under the poverty line. The incidence of poverty varies across regions and area. The Northeast region has the highest poverty level and people living in rural areas were poorer compared to those in the urban areas.

It is evident that the industrialization process in Thailand has resulted in higher income levels for the Thai people. As the rate of income growth has been higher than the rate of inflation, the real income of the people has increased over time. It is not possible to estimate precisely to what extent industrialization has contributed to higher income levels, but the average income of workers in the manufacturing sector increased much overtime as the share of this sector in GDP has increased, while that of the labour force in this sector increased at less rapid rates. Per capita product in the manufacturing sector is now many times higher than that in the agricultural sector, and the wages paid in the manufacturing sector is much higher than those in the agricultural sector.

The disparity in incomes of people in different economic sectors also reflects unequal income distribution. Like many other developing countries, the distribution of income in Thailand is highly uneven and it tends to worsen over time. The share of income of the people in the top decile was 34.6 per cent and that of the lowest-income decile was only 2.2 per cent in 2000. The Gini coefficient estimated by the National Statistical Office (NSO) was 0.429 in 1990, and increased to 0.439 in 2000 and declined to 0.428 in 2003. The average income of people living in different regions of the country also shows large disparity.

The industrial policies in Thailand have contributed to more income inequality as investment incentives and protection measures, up until the present time, have been biased in favour of large and modern enterprises. In addition, the rate of return of producers in the manufacturing sector has been much higher than that in the agricultural sector. The concentration of industrial activities in Bangkok and its nearby provinces also contributed to the regional disparity in incomes, and

Greater Bangkok has been able to extract resources from the rural agricultural sector. Productive workers have also been channeled from the agricultural to industrial sectors.

Industrialization has resulted in increasing employment in the manufacturing sector. Because of higher incomes in urban nonagricultural sectors, there has been migration of workers to urban areas, particularly to the Greater Bangkok region. As industrialization proceeds, the share of labour engaged in agriculture has declined while that of non-agricultural sectors has increased over time. In 1960, over 80 per cent of the country's labour forces were in agricultural sector. The share has reduced to 64 per cent in 1990, and further reduced to 48.8 per cent in 2000. However, the transformation of the economy has been less rapid in employment than in output and exports. For education background, more than half of the total workforce in the manufacturing sector receives only primary education or less. However, the average educational attainment of manufacturing workers tend to show improvement in recent years.

The above discussion reflects the country's weightage on industry and manufacturing so also the demand for labour in that sector compared to the traditional agriculture sector. It is also clear that Thailand's economy is primarily export oriented and that is possible only due to the high industrial growth. So far the industrial policies described above have been growth promoting. But in this context the trade policies are also in place. We now briefly review the important trade policies and measures adopted by the Thai government from the 1980s onwards.

TRADE POLICIES AND MEASURES[1]

Import substitution was the main objective of the Thai trade history since the 1970s to promote industrialization. The use of tariff was the major instrument to influence the country's development path and it effectively began in 1974 to promote domestic industry. The export promotion was more effective in the late 1980s. The main thrust was to promote exports, deter imports and curtail balance of payments deficit since 1981. In this regard the Exchange Rate Adjustment Policy in 1981(the government devalued the baht against the US dollar twice, a depreciation of 8.7 per cent) was therefore conceived as a means of boosting exports while dissuading imports.

The Export Promotion Measures in 1981 was to encourage exports of major commodities:

(a) The Foreign Trade Department announced a reduction in export premium for all kinds of rice by approximately 40 per cent.

(b) The Customs Department assessed price of rice for determination of export duty which lessened the tax burden to be borne by exporters.

(c) The customs duties on rubber exports were reduced.

The Ministry of Commerce enforced measures to increase maize exports by allocating and raised export quotas for the general market. The Foreign Trade Department lifted the levy paid to the Tapioca Price Support Fund. The tin royalty was reduced by approximately 12-23 per cent.

1. Measures to Safeguard Domestic Industries: Import surcharges were imposed at rates between 5- 30 per cent on viscose rayon fibre and discontinuous polyester fibre, polyester filament yarn, piston ring, diesel piston engine, purified oleaginous palm oil, telephone set, and certain chemical substances, etc. Licensing requirement was imposed on diesel engine, compressor for air-conditioner, potato, jute and garlic.
2. Measures to Slow down Oil Imports: Domestic retail prices of petroleum products were increased twice in order to reduce oil consumption, retail prices of all

kinds of petroleum products were increased on average by 18.2 per cent, price of premium benzene was raised by 13 per cent. In addition, oil conservation measures were adopted, notably the speed limit for private automobiles, adjustments in tax structures for private automobiles based on engine capacity, recommendations for more economical and effective consumption of energy in factories.

The export measure in 1982 is primarily based on the streamlining of export procedures:

(a) Tax measures: In the promotion of wood product exports, taxes on all kinds of wood products were waved from October 1982.

(b) Promotion of specific exports: Rice measures are undertaken to promote and accelerate rice exports. Major changes in the regulations on maize trading. The exports of textile and textile products to the United State were promoted further by requiring the stamp of "Textile visa" on such products and abolishing the control on certain textile products exported to this country. Certain export items, namely, cement, iron rod, vegetable oil, wood-free paper, newsprint, all types of craft paper, coconut sugar could be exported without official permission under the relaxed export control policy. Furthermore, the allocation of coffee export quota was abolished and free exports of coffee were allowed.

Import measures in 1982 are

Safeguard measures: The government imposed various measures to protect local manufactures. Licensing was imposed on certain import items for example, marble of some types, porcelain dining ware, copra, soybeans, soybean and palm oils, fish meals, used iron or steel containers for liquefied petroleum gas, two-wheeled walking and used 4-wheeled tractors, refrigerator compressor, jute and diesel engine.

Import Relaxation measures: the Government allowed imports of some finished products and raw materials to prevent domestic shortage and provide assistance to local manufacturers. Imports of parts and accessories of compressors for refrigerators, water coolers or other kinds of coolers provided that the assembled products must be exported within the prescribed period containing the exact number of pieces granted this privilege.

Foreign capital mobilization measures: In order to attract capital inflows, the exemption of withholding tax on interest income received from both short and long term foreign loans was extended.

To promote exports during 1985 several measures are undertaken: a) to reduce export duties on rubber and exempt rice exports duties entirely to enable exporters to compete better internationally; b) to eliminate special assessments; c) to reduce the royalties on tin; d) to lower the business tax and the municipal tax collected from tin exporters to reduce the cost burden to tin producers and exporters who have encountered problems with falling prices e)to expand the authority of the Director General of Customs under the supervision of the Ministry of Finance to reduce the duties on raw materials imports used by export industries.

Some important measures are also taken place in 1988. Rice bran residues and other agricultural by-products and export of non-living marline products were exempted from business taxes. Import duties on rubber dams for irrigation were reduced. Import duties on a number of marine products were reduced or completely removed, especially those imported across border checkpoints. Business taxes on imports of gold sold to export manufacturers and on incomes from sale of products of such gold were exempted. Business tax exemptions were implemented on the gross value of passenger cars or buses. Only the value-added arising from the modification of such cars was subject to business tax. Import duty reductions were granted on imports of billets, which were intermediate goods for the production of finished iron and steel rods, and on imports of iron and steel rods for construction. The excise taxes on four categories of petroleum products were adjusted as follows: a reduction of the rate on benzene; and an increase of the rates on diesel, kerosene, and bunker oil.

Measures to promote exports and imports during 1989 are: Import duty on scrap iron was exempted while import duty on billets was reduced if being used in the production of iron rods for construction. The reduction was applied to all sizes of imported rolled iron rods for construction and deformed bars. Import duty on coke, and semi-coke produced from lignite or peat production was reduced. Import duty was abolished on all type of raw hides, skins and leather, and was reduced on tanned leather.

Polices in 1990 were based on several items: Business taxes on importation of fertilizer, pesticide and related substances were abolished, and import duties on urea and pesticide were exempted. Export duties on rubber export were exempted. Import duty and excise tax on imported cement were exempted to prevent shortage and to assist the construction sector. Import duties on compressors and refrigerator components were reduced to assist the cold-storage industry for semi-processed seafood. Import duties on maize and fish meal were reduced to assist the animal feed industry. Import duties on billets and certain iron and steel products were reduced. Import duties on machinery and capital equipment used in industry and agriculture were reduced. Excise taxes exemption was granted for oil and oil products manufactured by industrial undertakings and used as own inputs.

To conserve the environment, import duty on catalytic converters was exempted to encourage the installation of such equipment in cars. Meanwhile, excise taxes on leaded and sulfured gasoline were also adjusted. Business taxes and import duties on computers and parts were reduced.

Adjustment of the production structure and industrial promotion in 1992 are: Import duties were reduced on the raw materials used in the manufacturing of automobile parts, fully assembled passenger cars, jeep-and station wagon-type vehicles, construction, steel, cement metal pipes used in petroleum, chemical or petrochemical industries, parts and equipment used in the production of power supplies for computers. Import duties were restructured on steel products and chemical industry products for rationalization of the tariff structure.

Thailand joined the WTO Agreement in 1997 to liberalise the trade of information technology products, under which tariff measures are to be abolished, and non-tariff measures reduced or abolished. ISO Standard Verification Institute was established in 1997 to sustain exports at the international level.

To promote intra-ASEAN trade, policy of reductions and exemptions of import duties under AFTA scheduled for 1997 was adopted. Import duties were reduced on electronic parts and components that cannot be manufactured domestically or to be used in export-oriented manufacturing. The prohibition of cement exports was abolished.

Trade policy 1998 emphasizes on reducing import duties and exempting surcharge in domestic steel industry and certain type of steel products.

Ministry of Finance, abolished custom tariff reductions and reducing tariff rates for 196 sub-categories such that tariff are collected in accordance with value-added at each stage of production (Primary Steel Products, Imported Steel Products for Steel Sheet Production, Tin-Coated and Cromium-Coated Products for Can Production, Imported Steel Products for Electronic Appliances and Electronics and Automobile Industry and parts). Reduction of import duties on raw materials, electronic components and parts aimed at lowering production costs for producers was adopted.

Measures to support private investment in 2000 are: The government reduced the import duty for 542 items of primary raw materials, intermediate factors of production, capital goods and 73 items of others and provided funds for financial restructuring of SMEs. The measures to liberalise import markets in line with the World Trade Organisation (WTO) obligations were Exemption of duty, reduction and increase of customs tariff privileges for 23 items of agricultural products specified under WTO obligations.

For promotion of exports measures such as: a) exemption of value added tax (VAT) for the sale or import of gold, platinum, white gold, silver and paradium which had not been in the form of bullion for exports and b) exemption of excise tax for the goods used as raw materials or parts in the production of exported products are taken.

International Trade Measures in 2001 are as follows: (i) Export credit was initiated; (ii) commercial banks would grant credits for exporters based on their ability to export starting from their business plan proposals which will induce purchase orders; (iii) VAT exemption was provided for domestic raw material used to produce exported goods, along the same line as VAT exemption of imported raw material used to produce goods for export; (iv) the tax structure was modified for imported raw material in order to enhance competitiveness.

The resolutions to enhance export competitiveness are as follows: improvements were made on the entire tariff system, by adjusting the rate of tariff levied on approximately 5800 items within 30 days.

Anti-dumping and countervailing imported products were also initiated to ensure coverage and compliance with standards under the World Trade Organisation which are as follows: to amend and improve factors and economic indices used in examining the effect of anti-dumping on domestic industries; to amend and improve the floor limit of the dumping margin, benefits from subsidies, amount of dumping-products that were imported and amount of subsidized products that were imported.

The industrial and trade policies described above have positive impact on the economy reflected in the country's high and rapid growth especially in industrial and manufacturing sector and export. However there is other side of the story—impacts on the environment cannot be ignored.

A short profile of the environmental situation in Thailand is presented in the next section.

ENVIRONMENTAL PROBLEMS: AN OVERVIEW

There are numerous distinguishing features of this period (1980-2004). The environmental effects resulting from Thailand's structural transition from an agricultural to an industrial based economy become noticeable and evident. With the rapid growth in the industrial sector, without suitable environmental management, Thailand is encountering acute environmental problems such as water pollution (dramatic rises in industrial wastewater), air pollution, solid waste, toxic and hazardous substance disposal problems, inefficient natural resource utilization and rapid decline in forest cover.

The three main contributors to pollution in Thailand arise from domestic sources, the industrial sector, and the service sector. All contribute solid, liquid, and gaseous wastes. Wastes from these sectors can be deposited on the land, in the water, or escape into the air.

Domestic sources: Large urban centers have been identified as the main source of pollution in Thailand and

Figure 3.5: CO_2 Emission in Thailand, 1981-2003 (thousand tons)

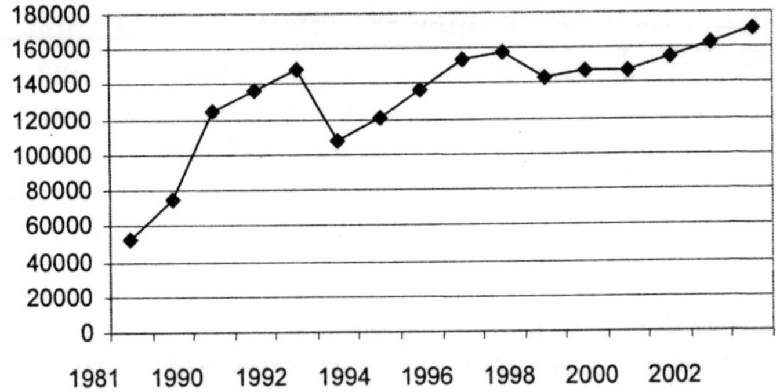

Source: DEDP (various issues).

as such, the majority of waste management efforts have been directed at these areas. In addition, hazardous wastes generated from communities are estimated at about 318,000 tons per year - which are not properly collected or treated. In Bangkok, hazardous waste collection and disposal poses a major environmental threat to its residents. The existing treatment facilities are only capable of treating a small portion of the hazardous waste generated.

Figure 3.6: SO_2 and NOx Emission in Thailand, 1981-2003

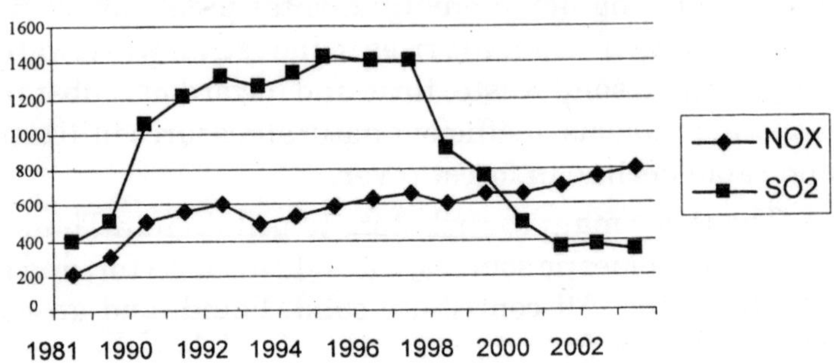

Source: DEDP (various issues).

Industrial sector: Over the past two decades, the Thai industrial sector has rapidly expanded, particularly in comparison to industrial development in other countries. Many environmental challenges have resulted from Thailand's rapid structural shift towards industrialization. The increase in waste and pollution levels, along with the lack of comprehensive environmental management programs, has led to acceleration in the rate of environmental degradation. According to a study in 1993 (Tesco, 1993), many modern industries including electronics and electrical appliances, metal and machinery chemicals, petrochemicals, cement and plastics contributed much to industrial wastes, and air and water pollution. The Central Region in Thailand accounts for 60-70 per cent of all industrial emissions in the country. Fossil fuel-powered thermal sources continue to generate SO_2, NO_2 and carbon dioxide (CO_2) and CO emissions, while, the daily standard for PM10 was exceeded 12 per cent of the time at the curbside monitors and 6 per cent at non-traffic dominated sites. The major sources of PM10 are industrial boilers (29 per cent), motor vehicles (23 per cent) and re-entrained dust from roads (33 per cent) in 1998. Industrial hazardous waste production in Thailand doubled from nearly 0.8 million tons in 1992 to 1.6 million tons in 1996 (TEI, 1997).

Traffic congestion and heavy concentration of industry produce significant air pollution. Every year, transportation activities produce more than 0.4 million tons of nitrogen dioxide and more than 1,000 tons of lead. There is also the problem of water pollution. Industrial effluents contribute to the pollution of rivers, canals and groundwater in Thailand. The 1997 water quality survey by the Pollution Control Department reported that only 14 per cent of surface water resources are suitable for aquatic animals and general human consumption, another 49 per cent are usable for agricultural and general uses, and the remaining 37 per cent are of poor quality. Marine resources are also dwindling as a result of water pollution and over-fishing. The coastal areas of the country have been seriously degraded not only by expansion of fishing but also by shrimp aquaculture, rapid expansion of manufacturing and tourism activities, coupled with the lack of controls by concerned authorities. Much mangrove forest area has also been lost and over-fishing has resulted in rapid depletion of fish stocks. According to 1991 records from the Department of Industrial Works (DIW), of the approximate 27,000 polluting-classified factories, 20,000 of these are included as water polluting. Industrial emissions indicate that Thai industries emit 34 million tons of carbon dioxide into the atmosphere, 0.7 million tons of BOD, and create 1.6 million tons of hazardous wastes. Consumption of CFCs and other ozone depleting substances by industries, was about 10,000 tons (TEI, 1997).

In 1992, the Electricity Generating Authority of Thailand (EGAT) introduced a comprehensive policy for environmental protection. Since then, environmental compliance of EGAT's power generating plants is working but hardly any improvements.

A number of recent studies have shown that air pollutants have increased mortality and morbidity, most notably in the Bangkok Metropolitan Region (BMR). One study reports that the Bangkok population has been adversely affected by increases in particulate matter - with an estimated 5,000 premature deaths annually. In one 1998 incident, 400 villagers were hospitalized as local SO2 levels of 2,200 µg/m3 per hour were reported (compared to standards of 1,300 µg/m3).

Service sector: The service sector sources of pollution are restaurants, shopping centers, hotels, hospitals, and other facilities used by the general public. Pollution generated from service sources include solid wastes, wastewater discharges (from human waste, cleaning products, and various types of restaurant discharges), and infected waste from hospitals. Another growing source of pollution stems from the tourism industry, which includes hotels, entertainment spots, and tourist areas. Normally, wherever tourism activities and services are located, as the number of tourists increases, the quantity of water used and the solid waste problems increase as well. The tourism boom is putting additional pressure on coastal and marine resources. The rapid expansion of hotels on the coastline, and ineffective wastewater treatment systems are degrading local water quality.

In addition to the above sources, there is also a close relationship between the agricultural sector, and the environment, especially in terms of the agricultural demand for soil and water resources. Although pollution generated from this sector is not as severe as that from other sources, it still must be considered, particularly in relation to the problems of water contamination and agro-chemical effluents.

Concentrations of biological oxygen demand (BOD) were almost consistently worse (higher) than the standard. The rise in ammonium nitrates in water is also contributing to endangerment of aquatic life. Groundwater quality has also been found to be inferior to established standards. In one study of 15 waste disposal sites, 11 were found to have heavy metal (nickel, lead and mercury) contamination exceeding standard values. It is estimated that more than 200,000 tons of waste (BOD) is discharged into the Gulf of Thailand annually. Industrial pollution discharges to coastal waters, the heavy metal count, especially mercury, has exceeded Thai water quality guidelines at times. Solid waste has steadily increased from about 30,000 tons/day in 1992 to close to 40,000 tons/day in 1997. This totals about 13 million tons/year, of which about 25 per cent came from Bangkok, 35 per cent from other urban areas, and the remaining 40 per cent from rural areas (TEI, 1997).

Industrialization in Thailand until recently had been based on the ground of lower production costs compared with more industrialized countries. The government was concerned more on low production costs and less on pollution prevention. As a result, the social costs from environmental deterioration had been ignored for more than three decades. As pollution prevention creates additional costs, manufacturers, including transnational corporations investing in Thailand, did not pay much attention to the environmental effects of their production. Trends in the ambient levels of these air pollutants can be gauged through appropriate and systematic monitoring.

To address this problem the Thai government took initiatives like other countries by enacting several laws and regulations. We will now make an attempt to take a stock of these initiatives.

ENVIRONMENTAL POLICIES IN THAILAND

The natural resource management laws have existed over a century in Thailand. The objectives of most of these early laws were to govern the resource extraction rather than conservation. The first environmental protection legislation was passed in 1975 before any other Asian countries. Environmental laws and regulations in Thailand relate to management of forest resources, water resource, land, minerals, energy, coastal and marine resources, industrial pollution, management of urban environment and community. This section, however, will briefly review the important laws and regulations for the environmental management of the country.

Thailand's policies and planning for natural resources and the environment was first specified in the Sixth National Economic and Social Development Plan (NESDP) 1987-1991). By 1997, there were at least three pieces of legislation in Thailand relating to industrial pollution, discharge of industrial wastes, and hazardous substances.

These are the 1992 National Environment Quality Enhancement and Protection Act (NEQA), the 1992 factory Act, and the 1992 Hazardous Substances Act. In addition, the 1989 Basel Convention on the Control of Transboundary Movements of Hazardous Wastes is the first global Convention designed to control international trade in hazardous substances (TDRI, 2000).

The 1992 National Environment Quality Enhancement and Protection Act (NEQA) Section 55 of the NEQA gives power to the Minister of MOSTE, to issue Ministerial Notifications prescribing pollution emission standards from point sources with respect to wastewater discharges, air pollutant emissions, and other discharges of pollutants into the environment. Owners or occupiers of listed or controlled point sources have a duty to install air pollutant treatment equipment or other devices for controlling, eliminating, or reducing pollution that could affect atmospheric quality. Similarly, Section 69 contains the same provision with regards to water pollution. Owners or occupiers of listed or controlled point sources are required to install wastewater or waste treatment facilities, or to send the waste to a central wastewater or waste treatment facility located in their area. As far as hazardous substances are concerned, Section 79 states that where there are no specific laws on the matter, the Minister has the power to issue Ministerial Regulations listing the types and categories of hazardous wastes that are subject to control. This waste results from the production and use of chemicals or hazardous substances in industrial production, agriculture, in public health facilities, and from other activities. The Minister is also authorized to establish regulations, measures, and methods to govern the storage, collection, safety precautions, transport, import, export, management, treatment, and disposal of such hazardous wastes by the most appropriate and technically sound means.

The NEQA contains provisions that enable those concerned to deal with or control discharges of industrial waste effectively. According to Ministerial Notification No. 3 (B.E.2539) of MOSTE, issued in 1996, wastewater discharge standards are prescribed for factories and industrial estates. The 13 parameters listed in the prescribed standards include the pH value, total dissolved solids (TDS), suspended solids, temperature, color, smell, sulfide, cyanide, various metals (including zinc chromium, arsenic, copper mercury, cadmium, barium, selenium, lead, nickel, and manganese), oil and fats, formaldehyde, phenols, chlorine, Biochemical Oxygen Demand (BOD), TKN value, and Chemical Oxygen Demand (COD).

Ministerial Notification No. 4 (B.E.2539) of MOSTE, issued in 1996, lists 104 types of factories under the Factory Act. These factories are subject to wastewater discharge controls. In addition, MOSTE issued another Ministerial Notification in 1996 prescribing emission standards for air pollutants from power plants that use coal, oil, or natural gas as fuel. The air pollutant emissions must comply with the prescribed standards and include sulfur dioxide, nitrogen oxides, dust, and aerosols.

The NEQA was designed to fill the gaps in environmental law enforcement where those government agencies directly responsible had failed to act. Although Section 82 gives extensive powers to pollution control officials allowing them to enter factory premises in order to check the operation of wastewater or waste treatment facilities, they can only take action after they have notified the responsible officials at the Department of Industrial Works and after the latter have failed to act. This applies in those cases where pollution control officials deem it necessary to issue an order requiring owners or occupiers of factories to rectify, repaid, or improve their waste treatment facilities or issue a fine. Therefore, by and large, the Department of Industrial Works still retains nearly complete control over factories. As a result little has changed in environmental law enforcement as far as factories are concerned. Ideally, pollution control officials, under the NEQA, should work jointly with officials from the Department of Industrial Works, but in practice, this hardly happens. In some instances, NEQA officials forward complaints to the Department of Industrial Works or its affiliated units regarding the operation of factories that have violated environmental standards or have caused nuisances to the point where they need to be rectified.

The 1992 Factory Act

This act together with the various Ministerial Regulations and Notifications issued under it regulates waste discharges from industrial plants. Section 8 of the Act authorizes the Minister of Industry to issue Ministerial Regulations in matters relating to the location and conditions of factories, factory building design or their interior environment, and to set emission standards and prescribe methods for the discharge of waste, pollutants or other substances that can cause environmental impacts.

In addition, according to Ministerial Notification No. 6 (B.E.2540), issued in 1997, factory entrepreneurs must also notify the authorities of details concerning the types, quantities, characteristics, properties, and places for the disposal of refuse and used materials, including the methods for storage, treatment, disposal, and transport of wastes. The wastes listed in the Notification include: substances that are flammable, corrosive, reactive, toxic, and washable: hazardous wastes from point sources; chemicals with acute toxicity; and toxic chemicals and chemical wastes such as those that are used as lubricating oils.

With respect to the control of air pollution emissions, Article 16 prohibits the emission of air pollutants from factories with the level of contaminants reduced to levels not exceeding those values specified by a Ministerial Notification. So far, Ministerial Notification N0.2 (B.E.2536) of 1993 has been issued specifying the quantity of 14 contaminants, which are permitted in air pollutant emissions from factories. These include dust, antimony, arsenic, copper, lead, chlorine, hydrogen chloride, mercury, carbon monoxide, sulfuric acid, sulfur dioxide, nitrogen oxides, and xylene.

The 1992 Hazardous Substances Act

It does not directly regulate waste discharges from factories, rather it provides for control over the production, import, or possession of hazardous substances that could become hazardous wastes in the future. "Hazardous substances," under the Act include explosives, flammable substances, oxidizing agents, peroxides, toxic substances, pathogens, radioactive substances, mutagents, corrosive substances, irritant substances, and other substances including chemicals or substances that could endanger humans, animals, plants, property, or the environment.

As far as the management of hazardous wastes is concerned, a Ministerial Notification from the Ministry of Industry was issued in 1996 specifying hazardous wastes, as listed in the Annexes of the Basel Convention on the Control of Transboundary Movements of Hazardous Wastes and Their Disposal. These wastes are deemed to be hazardous substances and the import, transport, and possession of these wastes are subject to control under the Act. However, no regulations have been prescribed so far regarding the ways and methods for the disposal of hazardous wastes. Regulations governing the labeling of hazardous wastes to show their type and properties, as well as, the required documents that would accompany their transport, are currently being developed. Persons who produce, import, export, and possess hazardous wastes are also required to notify and report the type and quantity of hazardous wastes in their possession in order to enable the authorities to check or monitor the wastes to ensure that they are disposed of in an appropriate manner.

The 1989 Basel Convention on the Control of Transboundary Movements of Hazardous Wastes is the first global convention designed to control international trade in hazardous substances. Thailand signed the Convention on 22 March 1990, and subsequently ratified it on 24 November 1997. The primary objective of the Convention was to reduce and control the trade in hazardous wastes. Thus, the Convention does not seek the elimination of transboundary disposal. The principles behind the convention are that industrial countries should try to minimize their production of hazardous wastes as far as possible, that disposal should take place within those member states which produce the wastes, and that trade levels should be reduced and should take place only with prior notification and by using environmentally sound management techniques.

The hazardous wastes subject to control must be packaged, labeled, and transported in accordance with international standards and exports are to be permitted only under conditions in which such hazardous wastes will be handled in an environmentally sound manner. No hazardous waste can be moved until the exporter has received written permission and the importer specifying that agreement has been concluded between the exporter and the importer specifying that such waste will be managed in an environmentally sound manner.

The Thai government has set up the Policy and Prospective Plan for Enhancement and Conservation of National Environmental Quality (1997-2016) and the Environmental Quality Master Plan (1999-2006) in recent years. The former is a framework for the conservation of the environment and incorporates environmental quality management plans. The latter outlines the work plan for different government agencies, state enterprises, and private-sector companies, and sets the implementation guidelines for environmental conservation at the provincial level. At present, several government agencies across many industries are responsible for environmental protection. However, they seem to have limited power to work independently and public institutions in Thailand are highly segmented with limited co-ordination among them. There are also overlapping functions and responsibilities among different agencies. In general, the implementation of regulations on the environment has suffered from lack of monitoring activities and weak enforcement. Information on environmental problem is still lacking.

This chapter provides a good overview of the Thailand's economic prosperity and growth fuelled by different robust policies involving industry and trade. It has also expressed environmental problems and the laws and regulations. Since the present study is dealing with the impact of trade on the environment so the proper empirical assessment is always needed to get a clearer view. Next few chapters will be focusing on the different aspects of trade and environment using an analytical framework.

NOTE

1. This section largely draws from Annual reports (various issues) published by Bank of Thailand.

4

Model Formulation & Data

The methodology of the current research is based on Leontief's Input-Output framework (Leontief, 1951). This is a method of systematically quantifying the mutual interrelationships among the various sectors of a complex economic system. The interdependence among the sectors of the given economy is represented by a set of linear equations expressing the balances between the total input and the aggregate output of each commodity and service produced and used in the course of one or several periods of time(Leontief, 1966). The structure of the model is extended and further modified in this chapter to suit the purpose of the study. It can be framed as:

$$X = A_d X + Y \qquad \text{.... (1)}$$

$$\text{Or, } X = (I - A_d)^{-1} Y \qquad \text{.... (1a)}$$

Here X defines the vector of domestic output and A_d the matrix of domestic input-output coefficient and $[I- A_d]^{-1}$, the Leontief domestic inverse matrix. Now the emission model can be formulated through (1a).

EMISSION MODEL

Total amount of an emission from fossil fuel combustion can be calculated as a function of output of industries.

$$F_{pd} = CL1X_d = C\,L1\,(I - A_d)^{-1}Y \qquad \text{.... (2)}$$

Here F_p is a scalar giving the total quantity of an emission from fossil fuels combustion in Thailand (Mukhopadhyay and Forssell, 2005).

Emissions under this study are CO_2, SO_2 and NOx defined as pollution type p. C is a vector of dimension m (1xm), of coefficients for the industrial emission intensity per unit of fossil fuel burnt. L1 is a matrix (mxn) of the industrial consumption in energy units of m types of fuel per unit of total output of n industries. In equation (2) CL1 carries only direct requirement of pollution intensities from industries and $C\,L1\,(I - A_d)^{-1}$ gives the direct as well as indirect requirement of pollution intensity from domestic industries. Let CL1 = S and $(I - A_d)^{-1} = R$. Then equation (2) will be

$$F_{pd} = SRY \qquad \text{.... (2a)}$$

MODEL 1 POLLUTION HAVEN HYPOTHESIS

To establish a link between trade and environment we need to develop the trade model by extending the equation (2a).

TRADE MODEL

By separating the final demand vector as domestic (Yd) and net exports we get:

$$Y = Yd + Yx - Ym \qquad \text{.... (3)}$$

Where Yx (nx1) and Ym(nx1) are defined as vector of exports and imports respectively. Here we assume identical technology (Heckscher-Ohlin-vanek) to find out the pollution content of imports for the rest of the world. So the pollution content of export and import can be defined as in (4) and (5).

$$F_{pd}\ \text{exports} = SRYx \qquad \text{.... (4)}$$

$$F_{pd}\ \text{imports} = S\,R\,Ym \qquad \text{.... (5)}$$

Equation (4) and (5) are scalar giving different pollution content of export and import. The sectoral contribution of the pollution (CO_2, SO_2 and NOx) content of export and import is estimated by putting diagonal matrix of export and import vectors which will become *Yx*(nxn) and *Ym* (nxn).

Now, a measure of **pollution terms of trade (PTOT)**[1] for Thailand with the *rest of the world* (ROW) will be derived by equation (4) and (5) as:

$$PTOT_d = F_{pd}\,exports\,/F_{pd}imports = [SR\,Yx]/[SR\,Ym] \quad ...(6)$$

Similarly the measure of **pollution terms of trade (PTOT)** for Thailand exclusively with OECD will be derived as

$$PTOT_{doecd} = F_{pd}exports_{oecd}\,/F_{pd}imports_{oecd} = [SRYx_{oecd}]\,/[SRYm_{oecd}] \quad ....(7)$$

This measure (equation 6 and 7) of pollution terms of trade indicates the ratio of the pollution content of 1 unit of exports relative to the pollution content of 1 unit of imports. A country gains environmentally from trade in relative terms whenever its imported goods have higher pollution content than its exported goods. When the pollution terms of trade are greater (smaller) than 100, then particular country's exports contain more (less) pollution than it is receiving through imports. The PTOT indicator has been used to reflect the pollution haven effect (Mukhopadhyay & Chakraborty, 2005). The expressions of (6) and (7) will provide the compositional effect.

Extension of Model 1

Model 1 estimates the pollution haven effect by the index of pollution terms of trade. The assumption of H-O-V has been made for that. In this extended model we estimate the index of PTOT by relaxing the assumption of H-O-V.

The present derivation introduces the emission intensities and technology of USA as a representative of OECD instead of identical technology and emission intensities. Keeping other variables constant the pollution content of import can be restructured as in (5*)

$$F_{pd*} \text{ imports} = S_* R_* Y_{moecd} \quad \text{....(5*)}$$

Where S_*R_* defines the total sectoral emission intensities of USA.

Now in this framework the measure of **pollution terms of trade (PTOT)** for Thailand exclusively with OECD will be derived as:

$$PTOT_{doecd} = F_{pd}exports_{oecd} / F_{pd*}imports_{oecd} = [SRYx_{oecd}] / [S^*R^*Ym_{oecd}] \quad \text{.... (7*)}$$

Like equation 6 and 7, equation 7* clearly redefines the measurement of pollution terms of trade. In addition to the compositional effect (expressions 6 and 7), the extended model (equation 7*) provides technological effect also.

The PHH explanation will be stronger if we discuss factor endowment hypothesis in this context, which offers another view on the impact of international trade on the allocation of environmental burdens across countries. This hypothesis maintains that pollution intensities of production are highly correlated with capital intensities (Copeland and Taylor, 2003).

MODEL 2 FACTOR ENDOWMENT HYPOTHESIS

The expansion of global trade receives so much attention largely because it has important influences on the factor markets of the countries involved. This also explains why, after decades, the Heckscher-Ohlin-Vanek (HOV) model is still a mainstay of international economics. The HOV model, which focuses on the relationship between production factors and trade, predicts that a country will export services of the factors that are relatively abundant in the country and will import services of the factors that are relatively scarce in the country. For testing the factor endowment hypothesis we have modified our previous equations by introducing labour and capital coefficients.

Recollecting equation (2a) the following equations (8-11) can be derived to estimate the total labour and capital requirements in exports and imports with ROW.

$$L_{exp} = LRYx_{ROW} \quad \text{.... (8)}$$

$$K_{exp} = KRYx_{ROW} \quad \text{.... (9)}$$

$$L_{imp} = LRYm_{ROW} \quad \text{....(10)}$$

$$K_{imp} = KRYm_{ROW} \quad \text{.... (11)}$$

Where, L and K symbol indicate sectoral labour and capital coefficients.

Similarly we can also compute the requirements of labour and capital exclusively for trading with OECD from the following equations.

$$L_{expoecd} = LRYx_{oecd} \quad \text{.... (12)}$$

$$K_{expoecd} = KRYx_{oecd} \quad \text{.... (13)}$$

$$L_{impoccd} = LRYm_{oecd} \quad \text{.... (14)}$$

$$K_{impoecd} = KRYm_{oecd} \quad \text{.... (15)}$$

As we know, the factor endowment hypothesis briefs that labour rich country will export labour intensive goods which are environment friendly and imports capital intensive goods. This can be indicated by the ratio of labour requirements of import and export which will be less than 1. Similarly the capital abundant country will export capital intensive goods and imports labour intensive goods and the ratio of capital import and export will be greater than 1.

MODEL 3 FOREIGN DIRECT INVESTMENT MODEL

The study has also developed a simple model to calculate the pollution content of FDI estimated through equation (2a).

$$F_{pd}^{FDI} = SR\,Y_{fdi} \qquad .... (16)$$

$$F_{pd}^{FDI}{}_{oecd} = SR\,Y_{fdi\,(oecd)} \qquad .... (17)$$

Where Y_{fdi} and $Yfdi_{(oecd)}$ explain the FDI from the rest of the world and FDI from OECD respectively.

The model has further investigated how far the FDI has induced the export and in turn pollution. For that FDI has been treated as an input in the economic activity of Thailand. The pollution content of export due to FDI has been derived as:

$$F_{pd}^{exp}{}_{(fdi)} = S\,R_{*}Yx \qquad .... (4^{*})$$

$$F_{pd}^{exp}{}_{(fdi)} = S\,R_{*}Yx_{(oecd)} \qquad .... (4^{**})$$

Where R* denotes $(1\text{-}A_d{}^{*})^{-1}$ and Ad* defines input-output coefficient matrix including FDI as an input. Equation 4* and 4** denote the pollution generated from the export content of FDI total (rest of the world) and from OECD respectively.

DATA SOURCE

The following data sources have been used for the application of the model.

1. Input-Output table of Thailand for the year 1980, 1990 and 2000 collected from the Office of the National Economic and Social Development Board (NESDB, 1984, 1994 and 2004) are used. Input-Output tables are Commodity by Commodity tables consisting of 180 x 180 sectors and have been aggregated to 50 sectors on the basis of the nature of commodities and its trade and energy intensiveness. Three energy sectors coal,

crude oil & natural gas have been considered. To estimate the extended part of model 1 the study also considered input-output table of USA for the year 1997(published by OECD I-O data section) as a representative of OECD. To make the table comparable with Thailand's I-O it has also been aggregated to 50 sectors accordingly.

2. To obtain the comparability overtime, the 1980 and 2000 tables are converted to 1990 prices by using appropriate price indices for different sectors collected from National Income of Thailand, NESDB (2003).

3. Energy Consumption data of Thailand for the year 1980, 1990 and 2000 published by DEDP, (Department of Energy Development Programme) Thailand are used.

4. Data on emissions of Thailand are estimated using the IPCC (Inter governmental Panel on Climate Change) guideline. The US direct emission intensities have been collected from CEDA 3.0 (Comprehensive Environmental Data Archive): Environmental input-output database for the United States (Suh, S., 2004 and 2005).

5. Data on trade with OECD for the year 1980, 1990, and 2000 have been collected from OECD publication (1986, 1992, and 2002). Export and import price indices have been prepared from Yearbook of International Trade Statistics published by United Nations (1984, 1992 and 2001).

6. International Financial Statistics (different issues) have been consulted for exchange rate.

7. Labour and capital stock data at sectoral level have been collected from the Report of the Labour Force Survey of Thailand, Report of the Manufacturing Industrial Survey of Thailand (National Statistical

Office, various issues) and Capital Stock of Thailand (NESDB 2002).

8. Data on foreign direct investment has been collected from Bank of Thailand (published and unpublished sources).

NOTE

1. This measure has been developed by Antweiler, 1996.

5

Results and Discussion on Pollution Haven Hypothesis

A pollution haven has already been defined as a region or a country with a concentration of pollution intensive activity that has been induced by pollution policy that is weak relative to its trading partners. Pollution haven model rests on one important assumption. Differences in pollution regulation are a key determinant of production costs and hence industry location. This has, as discussed in Chapter 2, been subject to much controversy.

In earlier chapter (Chapter 4) we have developed the model to analyse the impact of foreign trade on the environment of Thailand. Data requirements for the applications of the model are also reported. The current chapter followed by the next one documents the empirical findings on the impact of trade on the environment.

In this chapter the environmental impacts by testing the pollution haven hypothesis are analysed. First, we study the impact when Thailand is trading with the rest of the world. Secondly, the analysis has been focused when Thailand is trading with OECD, a major trading partner of the Thailand. Finally, tentative explanations have been presented for the impacts.

PTOT MEASURE OF THAILAND'S TRADE WITH THE REST OF THE WORLD

To investigate the trade impacts on the environment focusing on the pollution haven hypothesis we have used an index known as pollution terms of trade (equation 4.6). Results are presented in Table 5.1.

The values of the indices as displayed in Table 5.1 show dramatic change. The Pollution terms of trade (PTOT) reveals an increasing trend of the indices for all the three pollutants. As we have mentioned already in the methodology (Chapter 4) that once the indices are more than 100 then the host country is exporting more pollution than it imports. The indices of 1980s and 1990s of all the three pollutants show almost similar pattern having values less than 100 but with an increasing trend. The results do not support the pollution haven hypothesis. This implies that Thailand export goods that are more environment friendly than goods it imports. But the indices value is quite high above 100 in 2000 for all the three pollutants. For CO_2 it is 135.46 which represents Thailand's export is 35% more pollution intensive than its imports. SO_2's performance is almost similar with a marginal higher value (Thailand's export is 37% more pollution intensive) during the same period. In case of NOx the figure is little less than the other two pollutants but it stands above 100(25% more pollution intensive exports). Thus, Thailand is pollution haven in 2000. Now the question arises why Thailand is pollution haven in 2000.

If we try to explore the reasons behind the changes in the behaviour of **PTOT** over the period 1980 to 2000 in Thailand we need to look at the sector specific export and import performance and its corresponding generation of pollution. The most prominent sectors in respect of the share of exports and imports during 1980, 1990 and 2000 are presented in Table 5.2 and 5.3 respectively. From those

Table 5.1
Pollution Terms of Trade of Thailand with the Rest of the World for CO_2, SO_2 and NOx Emission During 1980 to 2000 *(KtC: Kilo tonne carbon, KtS: Kilo tonne Sulphur and KtNOx: Kilo tonne Nitrogen oxide)*

Emission	CO_2			SO_2			NOx		
	1980	1990	2000	1980	1990	2000	1980	1990	2000
Pollution embodied in exports (KtC, KtS, KtNOx)	12058.75	5303.27	21534.95	117.94	50.28	207.80	29.37	28.40	92.06
Pollution embodied in imports(KtC, KtS, KtNOx)	28984.73	10048.1	15897.55	298.02	99.06	151.96	60.17	42.94	73.39
Pollution terms of trade	0.42	0.53	1.35	0.40	0.51	1.37	0.49	0.66	1.25
Pollution terms of trade*100	41.60	52.78	135.46	39.57	50.76	136.75	48.81	66.14	125.45

Table 5.2
Share of Exports for the Top Ten Sectors in Thailand (%)

Major Sectors	*1980*	*Major Sectors*	*1990*	*Major Sectors*	*2000*
Food and food products	31.99	Food and food products	21.84	Radio TV set communication equipment	17.33
Non ferrous basic metal	9.39	textiles	15.28	Industrial machinery	13.68
Other transport services	7.90	Misc. Services	8.22	Food and food products	9.86
Rubber products	7.57	Radio TV set communication equipment	7.01	Textiles	8.02
Textiles	6.84	Industrial machinery	6.42	Electrical and Electronic appliance	6.53
Miscellaneous services	6.12	Other transport services	6.20	Miscellaneous services	5.15
Agricultural products	5.88	Jewelry and related article	5.44	Wood and wood products	4.67
Electrical Electronic appliances	5.30	Leather and leather products	4.83	Other transport equipments	3.54
Jewelry and related article	3.09	Rubber products	4.06	Other transport services	3.17
Petroleum refinery and gas separated plant	1.59	Misc. Manufacturing Ind.	3.43	Misc. Manufacturing Ind.	2.89

Source: Calculated by the author from I-O tables of Thailand

Table 5.3
Share of Imports for the Top Ten Sectors in Thailand (%)

Major Sectors	*1980*	*Major Sectors*	*1990*	*Major Sectors*	*2000*
Crude petroleum, natural gas	12.35	Industrial machinery	14.20	Radio TV set communication equips	21.77
Agricultural Machinery and equipments	9.30	Other transport equipments	9.37	Industrial machinery	12.04
Electricity	7.83	Iron & Steel	8.02	Electrical and Electronic appliance	7.91
Industrial machinery	7.70	Radio TV set communication equips	6.56	Crude petroleum, natural gas	6.92
Miscellaneous services	6.90	Electrical Electronic appliances	5.40	Iron and steel	6.53
Iron & Steel	5.64	Miscellaneous metal product	4.78	Other transport equipments	5.14
Electrical Electronic appliances	5.12	Agricultural Mach. and equipments	4.65	Basic Chemicals	4.56
Other transport equipments	4.75	Misc. Manufacturing Indus	4.17	Misc. metal products	4.54
Misc. Manufacturing Indus	4.33	Crude petroleum, natural gas	3.98	Misc. Manufacturing Ind.	3.61
Miscellaneous metal product	4.01	Food & Food products	3.89	Textile	3.38

Source: Calculated by the author from I-O tables of Thailand.

tables it can be seen that the composition of the exports have changed over time.

Before the rapid expansion of manufacturing exports in the 1970s, Thailand relied much on exporting of primary products to earn foreign exchange. Important export commodities until the late 1950s were rice, rubber and tin. Later on other primary products including cassava, maize, and a variety of fishery products emerged as principal export items. Since the late 1970s, the share of manufactured exports has exceeded that of agricultural exports. Processed food, textiles and garments were among the major manufactured exports in the 1970s. Afterwards more products such as integrated circuits, gems and jewelry, footwear, furniture, and plastic products were also added to the principal export list. From the 1980s, a number of electronic and electrical products including computer parts, air conditioners, and television sets have become important export products. More recently, motor vehicles and their parts have become leading export items.

Regarding the share of exports between 1980 and 1990 some broad similarities can be found. The most common sectors between 1980 and 1990 are food and food products, textiles, misc. services, other transport services, jewelry and related article and rubber products. The new entrants in the field of exports cannot be overlooked because the pattern of exports started changing slowly after the 1990s. The sectors like radio TV set communication equipment, industrial machinery, leather and leather products, misc. manufacturing industries secured a good share in the 1990s. These sectors have become more prominent in 2000 increasing their share in the total export (for example, radio TV set communication equipment share was 7.01% in 1990 but increased to 17.33% in 2000; industrial machinery increased its share from 6.42% to 13.68% during the same period; electrical and electronic appliances also secured a high percentage). It is implied from this picture that exports have become more manufacturing oriented in the 1990s compared to the 1980s and stronger in 2000 compared to previous decade. Food and food products deserve discussion in this respect. Being an agrarian economy much emphasis was on exports from this sector. The percentage of agriculture combined with food products shared 32% in 1980 and it came down to 9.86% in 2000. A major structural shift happened in the Thai economy orienting towards manufacture from agriculture.

During the 1970s, agriculture was the main contributor to GDP and its exports had remained the main driving force behind overall economic growth. From the late 1980s, the agrarian frontier went into reverse and farm acreage shrank (Pongpaichit & Baker, 2002). The population directly supported by agriculture dropped by almost 4 million. Agriculture's contribution to GDP came down from 25.4% in 1980 to 12.8% in 1990 and 8% in 2000 resulting in decline of its exports. This rapid decline was partly as a result of falling prices and faltering world trade. The revival of the Indo-China economies' renewed direct competition against Thailand's rice and other crops. Vietnam also emerged as one of the competitors in world rice market. Agriculture had a rapidly diminishing role in the economy. Once the export –led industrial boom began in the mid of 1980s, both public and private investment was concentrated in the urban economy to the detriment of agriculture. The policies supported the industrial take off directly rather than agriculture. By 1990, it was more than double of the agricultural contribution (27.3% against 12.8%). This role was taken over by the garments, electronics, auto parts, gems, light manufacturers, coming out of the new factories.

Several factors are attributable to the rapid growth of manufactured exports from Thailand over the last three decades. Among the important factors are as follows.

1. The availability of agricultural resources and low-cost labour enables Thailand to enjoy considerable comparative advantage in various labour-intensive and resource-based products. Processed food, textiles and garments, gems and jewelry, and integrated circuits in the assembly stage are examples of manufactured products which are either resource-based or labour intensive. These products dominated the export market in the 1970s and 1980s.
2. The change of emphasis in industrialization toward export promotion in the 1970s encouraged manufactures to shift from domestic sales to exporting.
3. Foreign direct investment in export-oriented industries has helped to generate new export commodities. Earlier, integrated circuits and canned pineapple were frequently cited as examples of export products created by FDI companies. More recently, computer parts, electronic and electrical products, and motor vehicles are all produced by companies with foreign investment.
4. The changes in international economic conditions such as the currency realignments in the second half of the 1980s helped to improve the competitiveness of Thai exports in foreign markets as the Thai baht was largely tied to the U.S. dollar time. The appreciation of the Japanese yen and the currencies of newly industrializing economies (NIEs) also induced substantial investment from Japan and the NIEs to relocate their export-oriented industries in Southeast-Asian countries, including Thailand.

Despite the various favorable factors, export expansion of manufactured products would not have occurred if manufacturers in Thailand were not eager to launch their products to the world market. Thai industries were rather heavily protected by tariffs until the early 1960s, when substantial trade liberalization took place. However, when the export promotion strategy was launched, many manufacturers enthusiastically responded to the government export promotion policy despite the protection made on domestic sales, and the modest export incentives offered to them. Realizing the limitation of growth in the domestic market, and the necessity to export for continued industrial expansion, entrepreneurs in the manufacturing sector made strenuous efforts to improve their productivity and product quality, and to find exporting channels so that their export sales could be increased. By doing so, they had turned export promotion policy into reality.

The composition of the imported commodities has not changed much. Import of crude oil and petroleum related products along with machineries are more or less maintained (Table 5.3). Analyzing the share the most important sectors observed are radio TV set communication equipment, industrial machinery, crude petroleum, natural gas, electrical and electronic appliances and iron and steel. An interesting point to be noted in this respect is the case of crude petroleum and natural gas. Thailand is scarce in crude petroleum resource. Its share declines from 12% in 1980 to 7% in 2000. During the period 1990 to 2000 the Government of Thailand has introduced various energy policies to restrict the import of crude petroleum. Along with this some alternative energy policy and efficient use of energy has also been initiated. Radio TV set and communication equipment gained much in its share (from 6.5% in 1990 to 21.77% in 2000). Electrical and electrical appliances also bagged a good percentage during this period. The electrical, radio TV, communication kind of industries has a favorable demand in international market which is reflected from the export share. The phenomenon of intra industry trade is observed in Thailand. For example, Thailand imports raw materials for electrical and electronic appliances product from USA and Japan and exports the final product after assembling.

For some industry Thailand acts as a component supplier but assembling for final shape is provided by the developed country.

Table 5.4
Pollution Embodied in the Exports of Thailand's to the ROW in 2000 *(Unit: Ktc, Kts, Ktnox)*

Major sectors	CO_2	SO_2	*Major sectors*	*Nox*
Gas and Water	3426.21	35.82	Textile	14.80
Petroleum Refinery & Gas Separated Plant	2797.17	29.18	Misc. Services	12.36
Other transport services	2651.89	27.09	Petroleum Refinery & Gas Separated Plant	6.91
Textile	1703.15	14.70	Industrial machinery	6.90
Misc. Services	1667.84	14.43	Other transport services	5.70
Industrial machinery	1424.51	13.53	Gas and Water	4.28
Radio TV set communication equip.	1208.79	11.20	Food and beverages	3.74
Petroleum products	994.43	9.85	Radio TV set communication equip.	3.72
Food and beverages	689.66	6.45	Petroleum products	3.30
Electrical and Electronic appliance	533.23	5.00	Basic Chemicals	2.91

The pollution embodied in exports and imports (Table 5.4 and 5.5) clearly demonstrate the reasons behind high values of PTOT for the year 2000. The most common sectors for all the three years are other transport services, petroleum refinery & gas separated plant, textiles, food and food products. Rubber product, miscellaneous services and transport equipments secured a high intensity in the 1980s but after the 1990s their values dropped. The pollution embodied in sectors like gas pipeline and water, petroleum refinery and gas separated plant are very high because the values of the total pollution coefficient (direct and indirect) are high though in terms of shares of exports these two sectors do not belong to top ten. The reasons behind the high values of PTOT in 2000 are due to the high pollution generated from the export intensive sectors. Changes in the composition of the export have a major impact on the environment during the study period (1980-2000).

Table 5.5
Pollution Embodied in the Imports of Thailand from the ROW in 2000 *(Unit: KtC, KtS, KtNOx)*

Major sectors	CO_2	SO_2	*Major sectors*	*Nox*
Crude petroleum, natural gas	3697.06	38.25	Basic chemicals	14.32
Gas and Water	1461.85	15.28	Iron & Steel	7.78
Paints, varnishes and lacquers	1075.68	11.25	Crude petroleum, natural gas	6.14
Industrial machinery	1038.02	9.86	Industrial machinery	5.03
Iron & Steel	1001.25	8.73	Textiles	4.46
Petroleum products	811.80	7.32	Radio TV set communication equipments	3.86
Radio TV set communication equipment	739.18	6.71	Plastic products	3.29
Petroleum Refinery & Gas Separated Plant	717.02	6.08	Paper, printing and publishing	3.10
Other transport equipments	612.44	5.84	Other transport equipments	2.88
Basic chemicals	583.03	5.31	Electrical and Electronic appliance	2.83

PTOT MEASURE OF THAILAND'S TRADE WITH OECD

The next attempt will be focusing on Thailand's trade with OECD exclusively. USA and the European Union are main trading partners of Thailand along with Japan. Pollution

Table 5.6
Pollution Terms of Trade of Thailand with OECD for CO_2, SO_2 and Nox Emission during 1980 to 2000

(KtC: Kilo ton carbon, KtS: Kilo ton Sulphur and KtNOx: Kilo ton Nitrogen oxide)

Emission	*CO_2*			*SO_2*			*NOx*		
	1980	*1990*	*2000*	*1980*	*1990*	*2000*	*1980*	*1990*	*2000*
Pollution embodied in exports (KtC, KtS,Kt NOx)	4120.11	2711.49	8579.35	41.55	26.14	83.11	9.13	11.76	35.47
Pollution embodied in imports(KtC, KtS, KtNOx)	8433.57	3014.48	5573.9	82.79	27.29	50.72	19.58	19.87	35.34
Pollution terms of trade	0.4885	0.8994	1.5392	0.5018	0.95786	1.6384	0.4664	0.5917	1.003
Pollution terms of trade*100	48.85	89.94	153.92	50.18	95.78	163.84	46.64	59.17	100.39

haven hypothesis originates from north south debate so the evidence on Thailand's trade with OECD will throw further insight on the debate.

Table 5.6 shows that during the 1980s and 1990s the values of PTOT are below 100. It follows that Thailand was not a pollution haven during the 1980s and 1990s. But the values of PTOT for 2000 are above 100 for all the three pollutants (i.e. 53.92% more for CO_2, 63.84% more for SO_2 and only 0.39% more for NOx). These results imply that Thailand exports dirty goods and imports clean goods. This finding supports the Pollution haven hypothesis. In other words Thailand's trade with OECD has varied implications for the environment during the 1980 -2000 period. In the 1980s the environmental impact was moderate but with the passage of time its severity has increased and by the end of 2000 the trade with OECD has created unfavourable impact on the environment thus turning Thailand into a pollution haven.

Why has this happened? What are the major commodities exported by Thailand to OECD? What are the shares and how far are they pollution intensive? We need to explore to provide reasons for changes in the values of PTOT.

Tables 5.7 and 5.8 record that Thailand's major export in 1980 was food and food products with 34.17% share which dropped to 9.97% in 2000. The orientation was more on textile, rubber products and leather during the 1980s and 1990s. Industrial machinery share has also increased from 4.21% to 10.09%. Apart from these, radio TV set communication equipment and electrical and electronic appliances together captured the market sharing 17.34% in 1990 and 38.78% in 2000. These figures reveal how Thailand has became an exporter of industrial goods with the passage of time with declining role of agriculture to OECD. Another most interesting feature of Thailand's trade with OECD is intra industry trade. It is one of the developing countries' trade features.

Table 5.7
Share of Exports of Thailand to OECD for the Top Ten Sectors (%)

Major Sectors	*1980*	*Major Sectors*	*1990*	*Major Sectors*	*2000*
Food and food products	34.17	Food and food products	15.85	Radio TV set communication equipments	24.01
Non-ferrous basic metals	16.64	Miscellaneous services	14.12	Electrical and Electronic appliance	14.77
Rubber products	9.90	Radio TV set communication equip.	12.44	Industrial machinery	10.09
Jewelry and related articles	6.22	Jewelry and related articles	8.56	Food and food products	9.97
Textile	5.83	Leather and leather products	7.25	Misc. Manufacturing Ind.	6.95
Agricultural products	5.75	Other transport services	5.85	Other transport equipments	4.45
Electrical and Electronic appliance	4.93	textile	5.57	Miscellaneous metal products	4.33
Miscellaneous services	3.29	Misc. Manufacturing Ind.	5.29	Jewelry and related articles	3.05
Misc. Manufacturing Ind.	2.67	Electrical and Electronic appliance	4.85	Iron and steel	2.88
Other transport services	1.57	Industrial machinery	4.21	Wood and wood products including furniture etc.	2.84

Source: Calculated from Foreign Trade by Commodities, OECD (1984, 1992, 2002).

The major sectors which dominate in case of imports (Table 5.8) are radio TV set communication equipment, other transport equipments, electrical and electronic appliances, iron and steel and industrial machinery. The pollution content of import items are high for other transport services, petro refineries and gas separated plant, radio TV set communication equipment, electrical and electronic appliances and industrial machinery.

The high value of PTOT (more than 100) in 2000 is caused by high pollution embodied in export intensive sectors (Table 5.9). The pollution content of import items for the year 2000 is shown in Table 5.10. Comparing the pollution embodied in intra industry trade (Table 5.9 &5.10) it is observed that values are higher for major export items (industrial machinery, radio TV set communication, electrical and electronic appliances) because of the large volume of export and its pollution intensiveness. It should be noted that the model has made HOV assumption.

Table 5.8
Share of Imports of Thailand from OECD for the Top Ten Sectors (%)

Major Sectors	*1980*	*Major Sectors*	*1990*	*Major Sectors*	*2000*
Industrial machinery	15.59	Industrial machinery	24.81	Radio TV set communication equip.	21.10
Iron and steel	9.40	Other transport equipments	16.73	Industrial machinery	10.41
Miscellaneous services	8.38	Iron and steel	11.69	Miscellaneous metal products	8.83
Basic chemicals	7.71	Electrical and Electronic appliance	9.75	Other transport equipments	8.17
Other transport equipments	6.99	Misc. metal products	6.97	Electrical and Electronic appliance	7.54
Misc. metal products	6.79	Non-ferrous basic metals	4.04	Iron and steel	6.96
Other chemicals	6.30	Basic chemicals	3.65	Basic chemicals	5.33
Electrical and Electronic appliance	4.62	Radio TV set communication equipments	3.46	Miscellaneous Manufacturing Ind.	4.05
Fertilizers	4.17	Plastic products	2.31	Jewelry and related articles	3.43
Textile	3.61	Textile	2.23	Food and beverages	2.94

Source: Calculated from Foreign Trade by Commodities, OECD (1984, 1992, 2002).

Table 5.9
Pollution Embodied in the Exports of Thailand to OECD in 2000((KtC, KtS and KtNOx)

Major sectors	CO_2	SO_2	*Major sectors*	*NOx*
Gas and Water	2224.79	23.26	Other transport services	4.92
Other transport services	860.85	7.98	Radio TV set communication equipment	2.78
Industrial machinery	693.44	7.08	Industrial machinery	2.45
Petroleum Refinery & Gas Separated Plant	493.85	4.96	Electrical and Electronic appliance	2.39
Radio TV set communication equipment	475.58	4.69	Miscellaneous Services	2.07
Electrical and Electronic appliance	454.40	4.25	Iron & Steel	2.00
Food & Food products	391.67	3.67	Basic chemicals	1.97
Clay and non-metallic mineral products	339.27	3.35	Textiles	1.85
Other transport equipments	304.72	2.91	Gas and Water	1.52
Misc. metal products	302.56	2.91	Food & Food products	1.49

PTOT MEASURE OF THAILAND'S TRADE WITH OECD BASED ON THE EXTENDED MODEL

In this section, we have investigated the result of the Thailand's Trade with OECD based on the extended model as developed in Chapter 4. As we have seen that Thailand is pollution haven in the year 2000, so the following experiment was applied only for 2000. Here the experiment is structured in a separate fashion. The assumption of Hecksher-Ohlin is relaxed in the present case. The sectoral emission intensities of US have been considered as a representative of the OECD emission intensities. The US emission intensities were used to calculate the pollution embodied in imports. The emission intensities of USA are in the unit of Kg of CO2, SO2 and NOx have been converted to Ktc, KtS and KtNOx for making the two systems comparable.

Table 5.10
Pollution Embodied in the Imports of Thailand from OECD in 2000 (Unit: KtC, KtS,KtNOx)

Major sectors	CO_2	SO_2	*Major sectors*	*NOx*
Paints, varnishes and lacquers	615.26	6.43	Basic chemicals	7.71
Miscellaneous metal products	494.92	4.76	Iron & Steel	3.82
Iron & Steel	491.29	4.28	Paper, printing and publishing	2.25
Other transport equipments	448.55	4.28	Miscellaneous metal products	2.17
Basic chemicals	437.20	3.93	Other transport equipments	2.11
Industrial machinery	413.51	2.99	Miscellaneous Services	2.07
Radio TV set communication equipment	320.15	2.66	Industrial machinery	2.00
Plastic products	286.93	2.60	Plastic products	1.87
Miscellaneous Services	278.83	2.46	Radio TV set communication equipment	1.72
Electrical and Electronic appliance	234.54	2.20	Textiles	1.45

The results presented in Table 5.11 show that the trend of PTOT remains same like the previous one (Table 5.1 and 5.3). However, the values of pollution terms of trade PTOT (Table 11) are quite high in the present case compared to the previous one. The values are 2.25 (125% more for CO_2), 2.79 (179% more for SO_2) and 1.41 (41% more for NOx). It ensures wide differences of technology and emission intensities between Thailand and OECD (USA as a representative of OECD). So the improved technology and lower emission intensities are responsible for the higher values of PTOT in the extended model. This findings support or at least do not contradict the PHH for Thailand in the year 2000.

Table 5.11
Pollution Terms of Trade of Thailand with OECD for CO_2, SO_2 and NOx Emission during 1980 to 2000 based on the Extended Model
(KtC: Kilo ton Carbon, KtS: Kilo ton Sulphur and KtNOx: Kilo ton Nitrogen oxide)

Emission	CO_2	SO_2	*NOx*
	2000	2000	2000
Pollution embodied in exports (KtC, KtS, KtNOx)	8579.35	83.11	35.47
Pollution embodied in imports (KtC, KtS, KtNOx)	3797	29.72	25.15
Pollution terms of trade	2.2595	2.79	1.4103
Pollution terms of trade*100	225.95	279.33	141.03

WHY POLLUTION HAVEN MATTERS FOR THAILAND

Several questions might come up in this respect. As it has been seen in the Chapter 3, that Thailand's exports shifted from agriculture towards manufacturing. Why has the composition of the traded commodities changed in Thailand? Why is Thailand exporting all pollution intensive goods at the cost of environment? Are the government policies not stringent enough to tackle these problems? To address all these issues we need to take a critical look at the government policies especially relating to trade and environment.

Thailand launched the first national economic development plan in 1961 with the import substitution (IS) regime to promote industrialization. The use of tariff was the major instrument to influence the country's development path. The role of tariff to promote domestic industry effectively began in 1974 by imposing escalation tariff structure where tariff rate ascended from raw materials to finished products. These changes increasingly favoured the production of finished products, particularly consumer products. The range of effective rate of protection (ERP) in the Thai manufacturing sector was between –20.92 to 236.43 per cent in 1971. This had increased to -

21.44 to 1693.41per cent in 1982 (Kohpaiboon, 2003). This highly distortionary tariff structure remained virtually unchanged.

Comprehensive packages of tariff reform were implemented after the 1990s. These packages aimed to reduce both the nominal tariff rates and different rates across products. The maximum rate had come down from 100% in the early 1990s to 30 per cent by the end of 1990s in most cases and lower rates for some 4000 items. As a result, the average tariffs have declined significantly from 30 per cent in 1990 to 21 per cent in 1995 and then 17 per cent in 1997.

Import substitution was the main objective of the Thai trade history since the 1970s to promote industrialization. The use of tariff was the major instrument to influence the country's development path and it effectively began in 1974 to promote domestic industry. The export promotion was more effective in the late 1980s.

During the second oil crisis of 1979-80 like other developing countries Thailand was also under pressure. From the mid 1980s Thai economy changed gear. The boom was driven by the exports of manufactures and services which grew almost six fold in six years. Major Japanese firms had transferred production processes to Thailand, in the later half of the 1980s. Foreign investment into Thailand accelerated dramatically from 1988-90. The first stage of growth in export industries was mostly focused in labour intensive and resource based industries and led by domestic or joint venture with Thai farms which had originally been established to supply the domestic market. By the end of the decade, foreign investment had begun to change the export mix towards technology based products. Textile firms from Japan and garments firms from Hong Kong and Taiwan had relocated production to Thailand and other overseas sites since the 1970s. These firms are highly pollution intensive. Garments firm expanded their production in Thailand not only to reduce production costs but also to find a way around the US general system of preference scheme which placed restrictive quotas on imports from individual countries. Several major gem and diamond cutting businesses relocated to Thailand. Over half of the total export increased after the 1990s basically from technology based industries, especially automotive parts, computer parts and electrical goods. These industries are highly pollution intensive (Lucas et al.1992). All big giant firms are setting up their industries in Thailand. By the late 1990s Thailand had become one of the world's largest assemblers of computer disk drives, and emerging as a regional centre for auto manufacture. The three sub sectors of automotive, electrical goods and computer parts contributed over a third of total exports. Above trade history reflects that how all pollution intensive industries relocated to Thailand. Actually Thailand always follows the strategy of "grow first clean up later".

The most proactive and ambitious trade policies of Thailand have changed the structure of the economy as well as export. Thailand has aggressively pushed to increase its share of the world's export market by means of establishing a healthy collection of bilateral as well as regional free trade agreements (FTAs) with its trading partners. USA exports to Thailand are particularly important since Thailand has consistently shown a trade surplus against that country. In this connection it should be mentioned that the only country to have completed a comprehensive free trade agreement with Thailand so far is Australia.

Thailand signed the GATT-WTO protocol concluding the Uruguay round, which included a commitment to liberalize trade in services. The development of NAFTA has had an impact on Thai trade patterns with the US. While Thailand has access to a larger market (US, Canada and Mexico), it also faces increased price competition from

Mexico in some product lines. Another issue affecting Thai exports is the use of antidumping measures and countervailing duties on Thai products, as initiated by US producers and carried out by US government. US investment has brought in significant technology transfer which has created a great impact on the Thai economy (particularly in computer and parts, computer software gas and oil development, refineries, petro chemicals and a variety of service industries such as banking and insurance). The US has been trying to secure greater market access in regard to services.

Import licensing in Thailand has been reduced significantly, but non-automatic licensing continues to apply to a number of imports. A number of products such as liquefied petroleum gas, kerosene, motorcycles and certain buses, are subject to import prohibitions. A number of measures have been implemented toward improving trade and investment relations between Thailand and the EU under the Asia-Europe Investment Promotion Action Plan (ASEM) umbrella, released in July 1997. This plan aims to promote public and private sector co-operation on the issue of removing trade and investment barriers between the two regions. Further, a 'Free Trade Area' under an ASEAN framework was initiated by Thailand in June 1991 with the goal of integrating production structures toward improving ASEAN's export outlook in the world market. The chief tool used is the Common Effective Preferential Tariff (CEPT) scheme, which initially targets the removal of tariff barriers *and* the *Framework Agreement on Enhancing ASEAN Economic Cooperation.* As a bilateral approach to free trade, an FTA makes it possible to abolish internal tariffs between the two participating parties, and thus, also makes possible further market integration. Having laid the foundations for achieving tariff liberalisation, ASEAN countries have been looking to reduce non-tariff barriers. Thailand's bilateral FTA approach (1999) initiated FTAs with Australia, Chile, the Czech Republic, Croatia, and South Korea. Thailand has been an ardent supporter of trade liberalization and Thai Government viewed the WTO as the binding and supreme organ of global trade, while AFTA is viewed as the mechanism for a regional Free Trade arrangement.

Nonetheless, in order to get the maximum benefits from and minimize the possible losses generated by the WTO process, it seems that Thailand has positioned AFTA as the most important mechanism in its international economic policy. The following few important measures have been taken by the Government of Thailand after the 1980s to implement the major trade policies.

Trade Measures of Thailand during 1980-2000

1981	✓ Reduction in export duties on rubber
	✓ Rice premium
	✓ Reduce the Tin royalty
	✓ Lifting of export quota
1984	✓ Devaluation of baht
	✓ Customs tariff were increased
	✓ Reduced import of luxury goods
	✓ Export duty was exempted for wood products, Para rubber, leather, scrap and waste metals, fish meal and dry fish
1985	✓ Exempt rice export duties
	✓ Reduce duties on raw materials imports used by export industries
1986	✓ Protected measure to promote domestic production of various machinery Business tax exemption was stoppedü Import duty was increased
	✓ export promotion encouraged again
1988	✓ business tax were exempted from exports of agricultural products and also tin
	✓ Import duties on number of intermediate products (billets) were reduced
1990	✓ business taxes on export of 15 agricultural products were exempted for one year
	✓ Import duties on compressor and refrigerator components were reduced to assist cold storage industries
1991	✓ Export duties were exempted in case of raw silk and garments

1992 ✓ Import duties were reduced on several items, raw material used in manufacturing of automobile parts, engines, passenger car, steel and steel product, cement, metal pipe

1994 ✓ Rationalization of tariff system

✓ The average import tariffs have declined significantly from 30.24 per cent in 1990 to 21 per cent in 1995 and then 17.01 per cent in 1997. These reductions were negotiated under the Uruguay round.

✓ Streamlining the tariff structure from 39 rates to only 6 rates

1995 ✓ Important measure to deregulate the manufacturing sectorü Petrochemical industry, petroleum industry, telecommunication power generation

1996 ✓ Value added tax rebate to the exporters, promotion of investment on manufacturing industries with strong export potentials such as automobile and parts

1997 ✓ Prevention of unfair foreign competition

✓ Antidumping surcharges on steel and float glass

✓ Some measures for Industrial protection

✓ Establishing ISO verification institute

✓ Measures for investment promotion and infrastructural development

✓ Import duty exempted on communication items, electronic parts and components used for export oriented manufacturing

✓ Qualification set for the exporters of frozen fish were abolished in accordance with free trade policies

✓ Prohibition of export has been abolished

✓ Extension of export credit by the BOT via the export-import bank of Thailand was increased by 7000 million baht

1998 ✓ Tariff reduction on steel products necessary for electronics appliances

✓ Reduction of import duties on electronic components and parts

1999 ✓ Measure to reduce the effect from the termination of GSP by EU

2000 ✓ Govt. reduced the import duty for 542 items of primary raw materials, intermediate factors of production, capital goods and 73 items of others.

✓ Measures to liberalize import markets in line with the WTO obligations.

✓ Exemption of VAT for the sale or import of jewelry, exemption of excise tax for the goods used as inputs for the production of exported products.

Source: Bank of Thailand, Various Annual Reports.

The above discussed trade strategies and policies relating to trade liberalization helped Thailand to diversify and boost export and also the economy, however, not favourable for the environment. This process has further been aggravated by weak and non compliance of environmental regulation. Let us now take a look at the environmental regulations.

To combat the environmental deterioration from trade oriented growth several environmental legislations were introduced in the past years. (For detail see Chapter 3).

Natural resource management laws in Thailand have existed for over a century (TDRI, 2000). Most of the early laws were aimed at governing the resource use rather than conservation. The first environmental protection legislation was passed in 1975. However a more comprehensive environmental legislation in Thailand is the 1992 Enhancement and Conservation of National Environmental Quality Act (NEQA). The 1992 NEQA appears to provide for a strong command-and control regulatory framework to set standards and to monitor and enforce them. NEQA strengthens existing laws within a policy framework outlined in the Seventh National Economic and Social Development Plan (1991-96) which has emphasized the environmental standards. Another important legal instrument is the 1992 Factories Act which regulates waste discharge from the industrial plants. Similarly another act, the 1992 Hazardous Substances Act provides control over the production, import and export or possession of hazardous substances that could become hazardous waste in the future. To promote and initiate energy conservation among all parties the Government introduced the Energy Conservation and Promotion Act (1992). Further, in 1997 Ministry of Science and Technology has prepared a long term policy and prospective plan (1997-2016) for enhancement and conservation of environmental quality of Thailand.

The existing regulatory command-and-control regime, a major source of debate, is slowly being replaced by the introduction of market-based instruments. In addition, direct pressure from many Thai communities affected by pollution is playing a role in influencing the government and the private sector to improve their compliance with environmental regulations.

In spite of all these efforts implementation of regulations has been far below expectations. The State of Environment Report (TDRI, 2000) has made a detailed analysis of the reasons. In the past decade, Thai governments have passed various environmental laws and regulations of environment management. In addition, the State has invested in infrastructure and awareness-raising programs for the purpose of protecting the environment. However, the state of the environment continues to decline due to several reasons.

First is the institutional failure. The government institutions are not developing fast enough to catch up to the rapid changes in the Thai economic and social systems. Outdated institutions and institutional structures and practices are used as environmental management methods. Thailand has not created the legisla-tive or institutional framework to successfully monitor and enforce emissions regulations on point sources of pollution[1] (World Bank 1994a). Because of this, ambient environmental quality in Thailand is poor.

Second, the policies and plans adopted to address environmental problems in Thailand are primarily technical solutions. However, institutional solutions are more required. The 1992 National Environment Quality Enhancement and Protection Act (NEQA) Act grants power to the government agencies to exercise their authority and to enforce the laws effectively through medium-term plans. As far as the ministries, departments, and provinces are concerned, environmental plans are simply regarded as a budgetary framework because if the environmental strategies for the programs are not indicated in the plan, they will not be approved in the budget. Consequently, the problem of depletion and loss of natural resources and the environment cannot be tackled without institutional references. Owing to the fact that the law, rules, regulations, and measures to control and change peoples' and organizations' behavior are not reformed, the policy and planning efforts can function simply only as a guideline for investment.(TDRI, 2000).

Despite the creation of a central PCD (Pollution Control Department) in MOSTE (Ministry of Science Technology and Environment), monitoring and enforcement responsi-bilities remain divided among numerous agencies. EGAT (Electricity Generating Authority of Thailand) enforces emissions standards on its generating plants. IEAT (Industrial Estate Authority of Thailand) monitors and enforces standards within industrial estates and builds and operates centralized wastewater treatment facilities within estates. (Limanon, 1999). Thus, overlapping responsibilities for monitoring and enforcement, and limited resources to carry out these tasks, have made the functioning weak.

Most industrial estates have poor environmental records. A 1994 study of the environmental practices of 49 estates revealed that most were not complying with EIA (Environmental Impact Assessment) requirements (MOSTE 1997). Sixty per cent of the IEAT-managed estates were out of compliance with emission standards, (Limanon, 1999).

Third, environmental programs require the coordination of public relations, and the necessity of government measures. Environmental information dissemination in Thailand concentrates on providing information to the public and has not included coordination between different government agencies to systematically achieve a common directive.

Fourth, government administration is not efficient in its ability to implement new environmental laws and practices. Most Thai laws are ineffective in the environmental management because of they assign substantial powers to the executives by allowing the issuance of Ministerial Regulations, Notifications, and Announcements. Thus, the executives (Ministers or Directors- General of the Departments) have the power to lay or reset the rules. Furthermore, if they cannot promulgate or modify legislation, they can still influence those overseeing the implementation of the regulations. (TDRI, 2000).

Unlike pollution control agencies in Asian countries (Malaysia, Singapore, South Korea, and Taiwan), the PCD until recently did not collect and keep pollution-related data on inspections, compliance, and penalties. Even data it collected suggest that the DIW's (Department of Industrial Works) monitoring, inspection, and enforcement programs are not effective. For example, in 1995, the DIW inspected 5,213 smokestacks and 22,815 wastewater effluent streams, and issued 1,488 compliance orders and 190 factory-closing orders (Limanon 1999). Because this represents a very small percentage of Thailand's industrial point-source polluters, the DIW had to rely on the quarterly emissions reports submitted by the polluters. And of those reports submitted, almost all show that plants are in full compliance. These reports can hardly be accurate given poor ambient air and water quality (World Bank 1994a).

Moreover, Thailand lacks an emissions permit system, and the PCD continues to lack full legal authority to inspect and enforce its emissions standards (Limanon, 1999). If the PCD suspects factories of violating standards, it must ask the DIW to act. If the DIW fails to respond, the PCD has the authority to take action. In practice, this rarely happens. A recent World Bank report on industrial pollution management in Thailand states:

> Public institutions responsible for environmental management are highly segmented with little coordination among them. Compliance and enforcement functions are split among the Departments of Industrial Works, Pollution Control, and Land Transport. This has led to poor implementation of the National Environmental Quality Act.... [Moreover] current enforcement efforts suffer from inadequate procedures, institutional overlap, insufficient staff capacity, a lack of incentives, and weak monitoring and reporting capability (World Bank 2000a). Thus noncompliance is wide-spread. As a result, ambient environmental quality is poor (Kanittha, 1996).

Fifth, the government relies heavily on the most recent standards from the International Standards Organization (ISO; the standards are known as "ISO 14000") to provide a stimulus to environmental cleanup. The Thailand Industrial Standards Institute (TISI, 2000) within the MOI (Ministry of Industry) has been very active on the ISO's Technical Committee 207 (TC 207), which developed the criteria for ISO 14000 certification. But so far, this effort does not seem to be having much effect. As of December 2000, 302 companies in Thailand were ISO 14000 certified most are multinationals, and all but 24 were certified by others rather than by TISI (TISI 2000). The government's effort to employ internal and external pressure on polluters has been of very limited success.

Rock (2002) argues that the Thailand's bureaucratic polity, its technocratic broker polity, and its semi democracy—have been sufficient to forestall better industrial pollution management. Moreover, efforts to lean on leapfrogging environmental strategies (e.g., a community's right to know, public pressure, and external pressure) have not worked very well. The question is why?

Part of the answer surely lies in the fact that the success of the strategies tried by Thailand depend on a regulatory base, which must be provided by a competent, pragmatic, honest regulatory agency. Because this agency does not exist, it's not particularly surprising that Thailand strategies have not worked (Rock, 2002).

The development of the civil society groups in Thailand, particularly environmental NGOs, has not kept pace with the current problems. Environmental NGOs do exist in Thailand but their problems mainly focused on natural resource issues rather than industrial pollution. In the structure of governmental institutions in Thailand permits the use of veto power to thwart most policy initiatives, particularly those such as environmental protection that threaten business interests. This particular combination—business dominated democratic governments, weak environmental NGOs, and an institutional structure that works against new policy initiatives—does not augur well for pollution reduction in Thailand (Rock, 2002).

One of the major strategies of Thailand has been to encourage the private sector to play a key role in the economy. But the private sector does not always support and promote the environmental quality by adopting environmentally friendly production processes. Moreover there is no suitable Environmental Tax. Thailand proceeded to apply tax measures to control pollution on May 1997. Still, the December 2002 Environmental Sustainability Index, which was conducted by the World Economic Forum 2000 to show the state of the environment and how it is affected by human activities, ranked Thailand 46th out of 56 countries. Rock (2002) has discussed in detail the pollution management strategies in East Asia and comparing the performance of several countries (Singapore, Taiwan, Malaysia, Indonesia, China and Thailand) concludes that "to date, Thailand has had the least success in reducing industrial pollution and improving ambient environmental quality". Thus Thailand has the dubious distinction of being the only East Asian newly industrialization economy (NIE) without at least one important industrial pollution management success (Kanittha, 1996).

Let us discuss briefly the environmental regulation existing in OECD and other major trading partners of Thailand in this regard.

The stringent regulations of OECD are well known. For example, Japan for Protection of nature and biological diversity, has introduced several laws from 1918 to 2004. To address emission of particulate matters from vehicles it has enacted few important laws from 1967 till 2005 to meet the policy target. Government also introduced several laws for solid waste management time to time from 1954 to 2000. All these laws are implemented according to the strict guideline of CAC, market based instruments and social instruments.

There has been major progress with regard to establishing the stringent legislative systems necessary to address various environmental issues. Updating a highly regulatory approach rooted in the Basic Law for Environmental Pollution Control (1967) and pollution control laws such as the Air Pollution Control Laws (1968) and the Water Pollution Control Law (1970), the Basic Environment Law was enacted to clarify the purpose of environmental conservation and related institutional responsibilities.

In addition to the Basic Law, a wide variety of media-specific and nationwide laws or regulations which are in place for atmosphere, land, water and forests have been adopted and/or amended, and relevant institutional arrangements have been strengthened in the 1990s. The regulations are in general strict and well enforced based upon strong monitoring capacities. Such regulatory measures are widely and effective used to implement environmental policy. As the Second Basic Environment Plan (2000) indicates, the best mix of various instruments is essential in creating effective environmental policies. The regulatory instruments still play an important role in implementing the policies.

Apart from OECD another south Asian neighbouring countries of Thailand is Singapore, important trading partner of Thailand. Singapore was successful, from an early date, in integrating environmental considerations into the machinery of both economic and industrial policymaking. Though it does not belong to OECD countries it maintains stricter regulation. In 1972, the government created a Ministry of the Environment (ENV). Clean Air Standards Regulations were promulgated in 1972, and the Clean Air Act was enacted in 1975. A Water Pollution Control and Drainage Act was passed in 1975, and Trade Effluents Regulations covering numerous water pollutants were announced in 1976. By 1979, Singapore was well on its way to growing rather clean economy.

Singapore's approach is that it was predicated on building and sustaining a pragmatic, tough, competent, and fair command-and control environmental agency, the ENV. The pragmatic and tougher and tougher emissions standards were complemented by strong programs to monitor ambient air and water quality. To this, the ENV added a rigorous, honest and fair inspection and enforcement program.

By the early 1990s ambient air and water quality in Singapore was equal to that in the countries that belong to the Organisation for Economic Co-operation and Development (OECD).[2] Like Singapore some other Asian countries also have stringent environmental regulations with good governance and enforcement compared to Thailand which create differences in the environmental policies between Thailand and most of the other countries

Thailand is trading. Thus the state of environmental regulations and implementation in Thailand are weak relative to other trading partners and OECD. Lax environmental regulations and non-compliance have thus distorted the pattern of comparative advantages in Thailand. Differences in cost of complying with environmental regulations between Thailand and OECD and other countries (for example, Singapore, the major trading partner) have helped OECD and other Asian countries to relocate industries in Thailand.

Perhaps these are some of the reasons which can explain why Thailand is pollution haven in 2000.

Some studies like TEI (2000) and Jha et al. (1999) while discussing the effect of trade on the environment have pointed out that there are indications that the foreign companies are relocating their businesses to Thailand to exploit weak environmental enforcement thus using Thailand as a pollution haven. However, no detailed quantitative studies on the pollution haven effect in Thailand have been conducted. But this chapter makes a detailed analysis of environmental impact of trade attempt to quantify the pollution haven effect. This effect has been analysed in this chapter in three ways. The first and second attempt concentrates on Thailand and rest of the world and Thailand and OECD considering HOV assumption, while the third attempt relaxes this assumption considering Thailand and OECD. It is interesting to mention that the results for PH effect in three cases are similar for 2000. Overall, these findings seem to support or at least not to contradict Pollution haven hypothesis for Thailand in the year 2000.

In this connection it should be mentioned that differences in pollution policy are only one of many factors that cause trade. Relative production costs are determined not only by pollution regulations alone and are not an important determinant of costs (Copeland and Taylor,

2003). If other factors dominate to outweigh the effects of pollution policy on comparative advantage then trade may not concentrate polluting industries in countries with weak environmental regulations. Developed countries are relatively capital abundant compared to developing countries which are relatively labour abundant. Traditional factor endowment prediction would give a comparative advantage to high-income countries in dirty industries.

So let us examine whether additional motives for trade change these results. In other words, our next task will be to investigate the role of factor endowments in determining Thailand's trade with the rest of the world in general and OECD in particular during the same period.

NOTES

1. The concentration of total suspended particulates (TSP) in the air in Bangkok was 370 micrograms per cubic meter (mg/m3) of air in 1998 (World Bank 2000a).
2. Concentrations of smoke in the air averaged 2.3 ug/m^3; total suspended particulates averaged 34 ug/m^3 (Tay 1993). Both are well below the U.S. EPA standard, as are concentrations in ambient air of suspended particulates (48 ug/m^3), sulfur dioxide (19 ug/m^3), and nitrogen dioxide (29 ug/m^3), (PCD 1994, 24).

6

Factor Endowment Hypothesis: Results and Discussion

In Chapter 5, we explored the logic behind the PHH by studying models where differences in pollution policy were the only motive for trade of Thailand and its trading partners. This chapter allows countries to differ along another dimension and investigates how differences across countries in factor abundance interact with regulatory differences to determine the pattern of trade. While there are many other potential motives for trade arising from differences in endowments, technologies, preferences, and scale economies, we just focus on one of these—factor endowments. We do so because most of the pollution intensive industries are also capital intensive, and because the factor endowment hypothesis is preeminent theory linking cross country differences in national characteristics to trade patterns (Copeland & Taylor, 2003).

This chapter focuses one important key questions how differences in factor abundance determine the pattern of trade in Thailand.

EVIDENCE ON FACTOR ENDOWMENT HYPOTHESIS FROM THAILAND'S TRADE WITH THE REST OF THE WORLD

We now discuss whether the factor endowment hypothesis at all supports Thailand's case while trading with the rest of the world and also the OECD countries exclusively. We have estimated the capital and labour requirements to produce one thousand baht worth of typical exports and imports in 1980, 1990 and 2000 respectively derived by equations 8 to 11. Table 6.1 reports the results.

Results show that Thailand seems to have been endowed with more capital per worker in 2000. HOV theory predicts that country endowed with more capital will export capital intensive goods and imports labour intensive one. It is reflected that Thailand's export required more capital (more capital per worker) than imports. More specifically Thailand's import is 13% less capital intensive than its exports. We also observed from the results that Thailand imports were 16% and 21% more capital intensive than its exports in 1980 and 1990 respectively. Thailand is a labour surplus developing economy which explains the higher values of labour intensity in the export basket of the 1980s and 1990s. But change in the composition of exports has reversed the factor intensity and a different picture emerged in 2000. Results thus do not confirm the validity of the FEH in case of Thailand for the year 2000 while it does for 1980 and 1990.

EVIDENCE ON FACTOR ENDOWMENT HYPOTHESIS FROM THAILAND'S TRADE WITH OECD

In case of OECD the labour and capital requirements in export and imported goods show quite similar picture like Thailand's trade with the rest of the world. Only differences observed are that import is 5% less capital intensive than its export in 2000 (Table 6.2). But in 1980 and 1990 imports are 33% and 20% more capital intensive respectively. Thus

Table 6.1
Capital and Labour Requirements in Exports and Imports (Thailand and the Rest of the World)

	1980		*1990*		*2000*	
	Capital requirements per thousand Thai baht of output	Labour requirements per thousand Thai baht of output	Capital requirements per thousand Thai baht of output	Labour requirements per thousand Thai baht of output	Capital requirements per thousand Thai baht of output	Labour requirements per thousand Thai baht of output
Exports	Akx = 626012293.2	Alx = 4637415.28	Akx = 1448895354	Alx = 4955519.688	Akx = 4838297426	Alx = 5023722.017
Imports	Akm = 956738455.2	Alm = 6104162.279	Akm = 990857723.9	Alm = 2777839.304	Akm = 2590823674	Alm = 3057995.087

1980
K_x = Akx/Alx = 134.99
K_m = Akm/Alm =156.73
K_m = 1.16 Kx

1990
K_x = Akx/Alx = 292.38
K_m = Akm/Alm = 356.70
K_m = 1.21 Kx

2000
K_x = Akx/Alx = 963.09
Km = Akm/Alm = 847.22
K_m = 0.87Kx

Here Akx = capital requirements in export
Akm = capital requirements in import
Alm = labour requirements in import
Alx = labour requirements in export
K_x = ratio of capital and labour requirements in export
K_m = ratio of capital and labour requirements in import

Table 6.2

Capital and Labour Requirements in Exports and Imports (Thailand and OECD)

	1980		*1990*		*2000*	
	Capital requirements per thousand Thai baht of output	Labour requirements per thousand Thai baht of output	Capital requirements per thousand Thai baht of output	Labour requirements per thousand Thai baht of output	Capital requirements per thousand Thai baht of output	Labour requirements per thousand Thai baht of output
Exports	Akx = 189003680.5	Alx = 1321655.8	Akx = 780161741.8	Alx = 1872121.8	Akx = 1713874498.0	Alx = 1792523.8
Imports	Akm = 273144212.6	Alm = 1432131.2	Akm = 530122021.1	Alm = 1057617.2	Akm = 1165240358.1	Alm = 1272383.7

1980
K_x = Akx/Alx = 143.005
K_m =Akm/Alm = 190.725
K_m = 1.33 K_x

1990
K_x = Akx/Alx = 416.725
K_m =Akm/Alm = 501.241
K_m = 1.20K_x

2000
Kx = Akx/Alx = 956.1236
Km =Akm/Alm = 915.793
Km = 0.95 Kx

the results do not support the FEH for Thailand for the year 2000 while they do for 1980 and 1990.

If we look at the north south trade we observe that developing countries are normally exporting labour intensive goods and importing capital intensive one. And according to the theory of factor abundance Thailand, a developing economy, is supposed to export labour intensive goods and import capital intensive. Thailand is exporting capital intensive goods in 2000, however. Thus, results contradict or at least do not support the FEH for Thailand for the year 2000 while they do for 1980 and 1990.

DISCUSSION

Why this is so. *There are many reasons for this shift in technology*. As already discussed in Chapter 3 and 5, from the late 1970s, and then more emphatically from the mid 1980s, the government shifted the economic strategy towards promotion of exports in manufacturing industries The shifting of exports from agriculture to manufacturing and from manufacturing core to the emerging groups is one of the most important reasons for the change of production technology—from labour intensive to capital intensive.

Table 6.3 shows how Thailand has shifted its export economy from labour intensity to capital intensity over years. During the first half of the 1980s labour share was more than capital while in the first half of the 1990s capital share is more than that of labour and in the later half it has been more than double.

Table 6.3
Labour and Capital Intensiveness in Share of Exports

Exports (share of total)	*1981-85*	*1986-90*	*1991-95*	*1996-2000*
Labor share	15.7	27.8	25.9	16.7
Capital share (technology based)	7.0	20.9	39.9	54.2

Source: Bank of Thailand, Quarterly Bulletin (Various issues).

By the early 1990s around 4 million people dropped out of the agricultural labour force in the off season, and around a million found other work, mainly in manufacturing, construction and other services. The largest growth in manufacturing in the mid and late 1980s was in the garment industry, the employment in manufacturing increased from 2.1 million in 1979 to 3.9 million in 1991 and 7.5 million in 2001 approximately (NSO, 2003). The transfer of technology with huge foreign investment started coming from OECD countries (especially Japan and USA) in Thailand. Industries which were set up after the 1990s in Thailand from other countries were generally large scale and capital intensive with less employment generation. Furthermore as will be seen from discussion the opening of such low cost locations as Vietnam and China undermines Thailand's comparative advantage in labour intensive manufacturing to more skill and capital intensive activities. The technology based export industries relied heavily on imported components, employed relatively few workers, and had limited linkages with the rest of the economy. The export sectors with high employment and strong linkages—agriculture, resource based and labour intensive manufacture—grew minimally.

Another motive reflects supply side factors, (Table 6.4) especially capital accumulation, which resulted in resources moving out of labor intensive agricultural industries into more capital-and skill-intensive manufacturing and services industries. In addition, trade policies have encouraged the development of capital intensive manufacturing, giving that sector an edge when competing for domestic resources.

The desegregation of export data by industrial sector reveals that manufacturing exports using higher technology continued to perform satisfactorily. In contrast, labour-intensive exports, such as garments, footwear, and travel goods, experienced sharp contraction. This indicated

Table 6.4
Annual Addition to Employed Labour Force 1980-2000 (thousand)

	1980-90	*1990-2000*
Total	805	216
Agriculture	345	-363
Non agriculture	459	579

Source: Labour Force Survey, August round quoted in Phongpaichit & Baker, 2002.

that Thailand had lost competitiveness in these sectors on account of rising labour costs and increasing competition from lower-waged countries such as China, Vietnam and Indonesia. (Pongpaichit and Baker, 2002)

The share of resource-based industries, including food, wood and paper resources, halved from 50 to around 25 per cent of total manufacturing value-added between 1975 and 1998. Labour-intensive industries, mainly textile, garments, footwear, furniture and jewellery, increased their share from around 20 to 30 per cent in 1990, declined to around 25 per cent by 1998. The performance of the labour intensive exports is not satisfactory. Practically all labour intensive export items suffer significant declines since 1995 (Table 6.5). The share of scale-intensive industries, including basic chemicals, fertilizer, refineries, cement, and iron and steel, remained stable at 18-19 per cent. On the other hand, the technology oriented Thai manufacturing sector made significant progress in upgrading its technology profile during the past twenty-five years. The technologically more-advanced differentiated industries, including machinery, consumer electronics and motor vehicles, doubled their share from 8 to17 per cent by 1995, while the share of science-based industries, including medicines, office and computing equipment, and precision goods, increased their shares most rapidly, from 3 to 8 per cent by 1995, and to 13 per cent by 1998(UNIDO, 2002). Since the floatation of the baht on 2 July 1997, the baht value had depreciated by 45 percent vis-a-vis the US dollar, thus helping to improve the international competitiveness of Thai exports. Manufacturing exports which accounted for more than 80 percent of total exports–exhibited considerable improvement during the second half of 1997, in particular those using medium to high technology, including chemical products, plastic products, computer & parts, and integrated circuits & parts (UNIDO, 2002).

The technological composition of Thai exports shows an interesting trend. 'Technology intensive' exports, which constituted over half of total manufactured exports in 1996 and grew at over 30% per annum in 1993-95, continued to grow during 1996. However, they suffered a slight decline in 1997 as compared to the second half of 1996. Since 'computers and parts' are not seasonal products, but rather products whose global demand is rising steadily and whose production is unlikely to be highly sensitive to labor costs. Thailand is one of the world's main centers for hard disk drive assembly.

In this context the following table (Table 6.5) highlights the technological composition of Thai exports. The technological classification of Thai manufacturing export growth and its distribution among resource-intensive, labor-intensive, scale-intensive, differentiated, and science-based products are presented.

Table 6.5
Distribution of Manufactured Exports by Technological Categories (%)

Thailand	*1980*	*1990*	*1995*	*2000*
Resource-based	21.7	13.8	10.7	7.6
Labor-intensive	47.0	45.5	35.8	20.0
Scale-intensive	7.8	6.3	7.7	8.9
Differentiated	22.2	14.1	19.5	32.0
Science-based	1.2	20.2	26.4	31.5

Source: Calculated from the commodity trade data base (UNIDO, 2002).

Since 1995, scale-intensive and differentiated products, followed by science-based products, held the largest shares of world exports in manufacturing. However, the science-based group was growing much faster than the other two since 1980, and is likely to become the largest group in the near future. The resource-based group was the smallest and slowest growing group. Science-based products raised their share at the expense of all other categories except labor-intensive products. Labor-intensive products grew rapidly (particularly in the 1980s) not because of demand growth or technological progress, but because of a massive relocation of production from high to low wage areas. In contrast, rapid technological progress and high income-elasticities of demand drove the growth of science-based (and, to a lesser extent, differentiated) products.

In this connection we can present some evidences of Thailand's trade with OECD exclusively. The Thai export patterns to the OECD over 1980-2000 is shown in Table 6.6 using the categories of low, medium and high technology, with resource-intensive manufactured products kept separate. Thailand's exports to the OECD are highly concentrated in high technology product. This is because the base of domestic manufacturing skills, supplier networks, and institutional capabilities play a very important role in competitiveness in technology based engineering products, for example, machinery and automobiles. In many high technology products, however, it is relatively easy to relocate the simpler labor-intensive parts of the production process in low-wage countries.

On the other hand, Thailand's capital goods import declined during the 1990s. Imports of the main capital goods for industrial investment, non-electrical machinery, continue to fall both in 1996 and through early 1997 (UNIDO, 2002).

These changes in the export and import market in Thailand have some impact on the labour market. Further the technological issues also matter for trade market as well as labour market.

What we have learned from the pollution haven effect in the previous chapter that Thailand adopted liberalized trade policy which entails a greater technological change. So the impact of trade policy indicates the changes in the trade market and it allows accordingly the changes in the orientation of the product categories i.e. shift in technology. This shift in technology finally is reflected upon the labour market through labour and capital movement.

Table 6.6
Structure of Thai Manufactured Exports to OECD Over Time (%)

Technology Group	*1980*	*1985*	*1990*	*1995*	*2000*
Resource intensive	59.3	54.2	35.8	28.1	14.6
Low Technology	22.8	30.4	39.9	33.5	20.4
Low tech less garments	11	13	19.8	17.3	15.9
Garments, textile and footwear	11.8	17.5	20	16.1	7.5
Medium technology	14.5	7.4	6.3	7.5	15.5
Medium tech less automobile	14.4	7.3	5.6	6.8	9.8
Automobile cluster	0	0.1	0.7	0.7	2.7
High technology	2.9	7.2	17.8	29.4	47.5
High tech less electronics	2.8	6.5	7.3	10	19.6
Electronic cluster	0.1	0.8	10.5	19.4	28.5
Others	0.5	0.7	0.8	1.5	2.7

Source: UNIDO, 2002

Tight conditions have prevailed in the Thai labour market for both skilled and unskilled labour during the 1990s. The problem of skilled and unskilled labour shortage has intensified in the early nineties. It can be easily clarified from the table below that job vacancies are always more than job seekers. Also the employment level declined from 1994 to 1996 (Table 6.7). In response, wages rose, with the minimum wage rates adjusted upwards annually at a rate exceeding the inflation rates. In particular, the minimum, wage rates in 1996 were on average 12.7 per cent higher than those in 1994. As a consequence, more foreign workers have been employed in certain industries. It is estimated that more than 700,000 workers from neighbouring countries are working in Thailand (Bank of Thailand, Annual report, 1998).

Table 6.7
Level of Employment in Thailand

Unit: Person	*1993*	*1994*	*1995*	*1996*
Job seekers	147,697	163,696	145,805	144,754
Job vacancies	390,145	560,403	458,421	430,494
Employment level	99,088	117,492	117,685	107,378

Source: Bank of Thailand, Annual Report, 1998

According to the survey conducted by Watson Wyatt reported in the Economist Intelligence Unit, the average wage rates of the foreign firms operating in Thailand were relatively high, compared with other ASEAN countries, but lower than Singapore and Malaysia. In particular, the wage rates of the unskilled workers working in Thailand were about 3 times higher than in Vietnam, 1.8 times those in Indonesia, 1.6 times those in the Philippines. The increased wage lowered competitiveness in certain labour-intensive industries, namely footwear, garments, toys, and travelling goods, whose export values also declined in 1996.

As a result of the higher wage rates, labour-intensive industries needed to upgrade production towards higher value-added and higher technology. This, therefore, has increased demand for skilled labour. The minimum educational level of Thai workers needed is the secondary level. However the workers lack this minimum level. Workers in the industrial sector generally have low formal education, while engineers and technicians have limited capability in the foreign language (English or Japanese) which is essential for effective technology transfer.

Thailand has a high literacy rate, but secondary school enrollment rates are low and about half of the students finishing primary level do not continue their study in secondary schools. A study at the TDRI found that in 1990, 83 percent of the workforce in the industrial sector are those with primary education or lower (Myers and Sussangkarn, 1992). Even with the extension of school years for children, in the year 2000, a majority of workers (more than 75 percent) in the industrial sector would still be those with primary education or lower, since it takes time for the high school students to enter into the workforce.

Moreover, the number of university graduates-especially in the fields of engineering, medicine, and natural science, which accounted for only 30 percent of total graduates were below the requirement level of the economy. According to the statistics of the Ministry of Labour and Social Welfare, the annual average rate of job placement was about 20 to 25 percent of the total amount of job applicants (Bank of Thailand, Annual Report, 1998). Such a relatively low rate of employment matching reflected, to a great extent, insufficient qualifications of job seekers with regard to educational background and work experience. Thus the scarcity of skilled labour has been a critical problem in Thailand (Phongpaichit & Baker, 2002). This posed a serious constraint for Thailand to move towards more technologically sophisticated industries and forced the industry to reallocate its factors of production and thus pushed the economy to use the capital intensive technology.

Thus the above discussion outlines important reasons of declining labour intensity overtime with increasing trend of capital intensity and hereby attempts to explain why Thailand's export is more capital intensive than labour in 2000. Further it provides explanation that why Thailand is supportive of the FEH in 1980 and 1990 not in 2000.

Reiterating the hypothesis again that countries with relatively abundant in factors that are used intensively in polluting industries will on average get dirtier as trade liberalises, while countries that are relatively abundant in factors used intensively in clean industries will get cleaner. As we know that the most capital abundant country has a comparative advantage in dirty goods and least capital abundant country has a comparative advantage in the clean goods. The predictions of this theory, therefore, sharply contrast with those of the PHH. In this context it is important to mention that the capital intensity will have a direct relation with the pollution intensity. It is established by a number of studies (Lucas, Wheeler and Hettige, 1992). The present evidence is also according to the line of the above arguments by supporting PHH and contradicting FEH on the same floor.

Our work reflects the implications of countries differing in both pollution policy and factor endowments. Since comparative advantage is determined jointly by differences in pollution policy and differences in factor endowment, most of the predictions of the PHH model can be reversed in a world where factor endowments matter. It is also possible that factor endowment differences may not be sufficient to offset the cost differential created by different regulations. The pollution regulation and factor endowment differences are the two important determinants of trade flows and pattern. Various empirical studies analysed these two motives in a different way (Chapter 2). Findings evidence that trade flows are primarily determined by factor endowment does not imply that pollution regulation differences are irrelevant (Copeland & Taylor, 2003). There is no clear cut consensus in this respect. But our results suggest that factor endowment effects of Thailand can reinforce pollution policy effect.

7

Foreign Direct Investment and its Impact on the Environment

So far the study has focused on the impact of liberalized trade on the environment and also on two hypotheses—pollution haven and factor endowment. In this connection we have investigated the role of environmental regulations, factor endowments, trade policies and environment energy policies and so on. It is important to note that impact of trade flows on the environment can also be influenced by foreign direct investment other than factor endowments and environmental regulations. We shall now discuss the role of the Foreign Direct Investment (FDI) in the economy of Thailand and its implications on the environment in Thailand.

The role of foreign direct investment has been widely recognized as a growth-enhancing factor in developing countries (Kohpaiboon, 2003). FDI enables investment receiving countries to attain investment levels beyond their own domestic saving. Further, FDI is an important avenue through which modern technology and innovation transfer from developed to developing countries. However, it is also evident from the literature that the growth encouraging effect from FDI seems to vary from country to country. Starting with the pioneering work by Bhagwati (1973), an extensive literature has attempted to show the impacts of trade on the gains from FDI to the host countries (Bhagwati, 1978, 1985 and 1994; Brecher and Diaz-Alejandro 1977; Brecher and Findlay 1983). On the other hand literature has also documented adverse impact on FDI on the growth process (Balasubramanyam *et al.*, 1996; Borensztein *et al.*, 1998; De Mello, 1999; Lipsey, 2000 and; Xu, 2000). In other words, the growth promoting effect of FDI is not automatic rather depends on country specific factors (Kohpaiboon, 2003).

Various studies have focused (Kohpaiboon, 2003 Pongpaichit & Baker, 2002, Pupphavesa and Pussarungsri 1994, Siam Walla, et al., 1999 and Tangkitvanich *et al.*, 2004) on contribution of FDI to the economic development of Thailand. Throughout the past four decades, Thailand has been a significant recipient of FDI among developing countries.

PATTERN OF FOREIGN DIRECT INVESTMENT (FDI) IN THAILAND

According to the statistics compiled by UNCTAD (UNCTAD, 2001, 2002), FDI flows in various regions of the world have grown rapidly over the years, although declined sharply in 2001 as a result of economic slowdown. On the average about two-thirds of FDI flows in the last decade went to developed countries, while developing economies as a whole received about one-third of the total flows. In the developing world Asia was the most major recipient region of FDI. Among the developing economies in Asia, the bulk of FDI flows have been concentrated in the countries in East and Southeast Asia. Thailand is among the ASEAN has been a preferred destination for foreign direct investment (FDI) in Asia for the past decade, ranking around fifth among Asian countries in terms of net FDI inflows. China and other ASEAN countries are also receiving FDI flows considerably.

From a historical perspective, FDI was a key factor in Thailand achieving one of the world's fastest rates of economic growth until 1997. The dramatic economic growth (as discussed in Chapter 3) was driven largely by increasing inward FDI flows. Figure 7.1 shows the trend of FDI flow.

FDI has been indispensable to the development of many sectors, particularly automobiles and electronics. As a developing country with a low technological capability, Thailand would not have been able to build up its industries to the extent that it did without FDI. In fact, like other 'Asian Miracle' countries, Thailand's success can be attributed to a combination of a favorable external environment and the country's ability to make use of FDI to transform itself from an agriculture to an industrial economy (Tangkitvanich *et al.*, 2004).

In the first half of the 1980s, FDI in Thailand was rather small and fluctuated dramatically due to instability in both the domestic and world economies. FDI in Thailand started to expand at an exceptional pace during the second half of the decade, partly because of the 1985 Plaza Accord, which resulted in a sharp appreciation of the Japanese Yen. This coincided with an increase in production costs in the Asian newly industrializing economies (NIEs) - Taipei, China; Hong Kong, China; and the Republic of Korea- making them less attractive locations for labor-intensive industries. Thailand became an increasingly attractive destination for FDI, especially from the Japanese manufacturers (The value of net FDI inflows increased twelve fold between 1980 and 1996, from $189 million to $2.27 billion, while the inward FDI stock increased from $981 million to $28.2 billion).

In this period Thai government switched from an import substitution to an export-led growth strategy. The success of the export-oriented policy can be attributed to a number of factors, one being the country's fixed exchange rate regime whereby the Thai baht was pegged to the US dollar until the crisis in 1997. Businesses benefited from the stability of the local currency and hence, that of the economy as a whole as well. Occasional devaluations (in 1973, 1981, and 1984) were carried out to ensure that Thai exports remained competitive in the global market. Other contributing factors include macroeconomic and political stability, the absence of ethnic or religious conflicts, relatively cheap labor, and strong work ethics among the labour force, coupled with an array of investment incentives. Among these, low wage was one of the key factors that prompted major industrialized countries to relocate production of labor intensive products to Thailand. This was made possible by the government's conservative minimum wage policy.

The value of FDI during 1996-98 was US$ 11039 million, showing a rising trend. The growth of FDI in the post-crisis period can be attributed to the increase in loans provided to affiliates, and to the dramatic rise in the number in mergers and acquisitions (M&As). The baht depreciation reduced domestic production costs and asset values, making FDI more profitable during the economic downturn. The more liberal FDI regime introduced as part of crisis management and corporate-restructuring packages (recapitalization in joint ventures by their foreign partners), also opened up new opportunities for cross-border M&As, which increased sharply during 1997-98. Further, some major commercial banks and finance companies have recapitalized and sold a substantial part of their shares to foreign investors, hence there were large FDI inflows into the financial sector after the crisis.

Actually the shock of the economic crisis prompted the Thai government to reevaluate its growth-oriented development policy. Structural flaws in both the industrial and the financial sector had contributed to the crisis. Compared with the People's Republic of China (PRC), labor was no longer cheap in Thailand Limited public investment in training and education had rendered industry incapable of shifting from labor-intensive production toward activities with higher value-added. The absence of a coherent industrial policy meant that industries were constantly lobbying government for piecemeal policy changes to promote or maintain their competitiveness.

Figure 7.1
Total FDI Flow in Thailand, 1980-2004 (million USD)

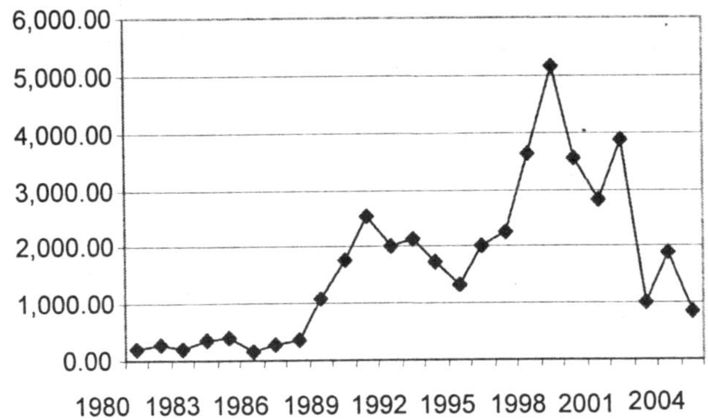

The flow of FDI is fluctuating after 2000. This trend is due to a result of both a fall in the size of gross inflows and a rise in size of gross outflows. The responsible factors are as follows. (1) The debt restructuring process that is slowing down implies smaller inflows of capital from overseas. (2) Low domestic interest rates due to ample liquidity have encouraged many MNCs to switch from equity investment to domestic borrowing, leading to low FDI inflows. (3) The competitiveness of Thai industries declined. FDI inflows into the manufacturing sector in the year 2002 were only a third of that in the previous year. Factors that are adverse to the competitiveness of the Thai industries include high and distortionary tariffs, high labor costs (compared with new ASEAN members and China) and lack of industrial upgrading. (4) The remittance of profits of foreign companies who invested in the Financial Restructuring Agency assets contributed to a surge in FDI outflows.

FOREIGN DIRECT INVESTMENT BY COUNTRY

Table 1 reports the FDI by different countries. It is seen that the top investors are Japan, USA and the EU in the 1980s. Then in the 1990s ASEAN enter into the picture prominently. Investment from Asian NIES, such as Hong Kong, Singapore and South Korea, grew rapidly. In addition, investment from European countries, the main target in the BOI's attempts to attract investment, also increased satisfactorily. Till the late 1990s the FDI was predominantly captured by OECD countries. The share of OECD countries during 1980-84 was 71.36% (Table 7.1) and more or less maintained its flow till the year 1995-2000(67.12%). However, during the early 2000 there has been a change in the shares (41.90% in 2001-4). After the crisis (especially between 2001-4) the US and Europe share decline significantly while Japan and ASEAN (including Singapore, Hong-Kong and Taiwan) became the dominant investors accounting for the 80% of total FDI. This change of share depended on the amount of investment and the pattern of foreign shareholding; for instance, whether or not a company was wholly foreign-owned or whether foreigners owned a majority of the shares. In any case, these figures indicate the sharp rise of Japanese investment during 1987 and 1989. Based on these observations, therefore, it may be said that the two leading countries investing in Thailand, in terms of BOI-promoted projects are Japan and Taiwan.

The pattern of direct investment from five countries Japan, the US, Taiwan, Hong Kong and Singapore-can be seen from Table 1. First, Japan, the US and Taiwan invest mainly in equity, while Hong Kong and Singapore concentrate on investment loans. Second, equity investments in the 1980's expanded, particularly from

Japan. Hong Kong and Taiwan are also growing rapidly as sources of equity investment. The increase in equity investment from Hong Kong is particularly noteworthy of its imminent return of China. On the other hand, equity investment from the US underwent a decline after 1984. Third, Japan became the largest source of loans as well as equity investment in the latter half of the 1980's, while investment from Hong Kong leveled off and Singapore marked a decrease after it had reached a peak in the first half of the 1980s. Finally, although investment loans consist of medium and long-term loans, those extended by Hong Kong and Singapore tend to be of the short-term type compared with those from Japan and the US.

Table 7.1
Net Inflow of FDI (million USD and %share)

	1980-84	*1985-89*	*1990-94*	*1995-2000*	*2001-04*
Japan	368.78	1608.97	2482.20	5270.93	3519.98
	25.72	43.94	25.37	27.14	46.24
USA	394.60	535.94	1382.69	4012.40	-389.94
	27.52	14.64	14.13	20.66	-5.12
EU15 5/	241.83	327.66	992.17	3498.34	-158.42
	16.86	8.95	10.14	18.02	-2.08
ASEAN 5 7/	132.18	166.38	1091.15	2287.09	3863.68
	9.22	4.54	11.15	11.78	50.76
ASEAN 8/	133.16	170.22	1095.03	2310.04	3881.43
	9.29	4.65	11.19	11.90	50.99
Singapore	113.84	161.32	1037.85	2118.07	3575.18
	7.94	4.41	10.61	10.91	46.97
Hong Kong	147.54	423.83	1829.59	1895.54	603.69
	10.29	11.57	18.70	9.76	7.93
Taiwan	3.84	359.33	608.23	755.08	381.95
	0.27	9.81	6.22	3.89	5.02
Korea, South	1.58	22.81	68.51	141.62	128.93
	0.11	0.62	0.70	0.73	1.69
Australia	18.12	9.66	102.75	252.78	88.95
	1.26	0.26	1.05	1.30	1.17
other countries	124.60	203.58	1221.86	1281.77	-444.26
	8.69	5.56	12.49	6.60	-5.84
Total	1434.05	3662.00	9783.02	19418.49	7612.32
	100	100	100	100	100

Source: Bank of Thailand.

FOREIGN DIRECT INVESTMENT BY SECTOR

Table 7.2 presents the inflow of foreign direct investment by sectors. It is observed that the industrial sector accounted for the largest share which has gone up from 24.10% in 1980-84 to 64.19% in 2001-4. Within the industrial sector, electrical appliances, machinery and transport equipment have a major share. Construction which was the attraction for the investors in the 1980s lost its importance in the 1990s and early 2000. Other sectors like chemicals, metal and non-metallic products, textiles, and food gained much importance.

On the whole foreign direct inflows to Thailand boomed in 1995-2000. It increased from around US$ 515 million during the period of 1970-75 to over US$ 19418 million during the period of 1995-2000. The share of FDI in Gross Domestic Investment (GDI), which was around 2-3 per cent in the 1980s, reached around 7.2% in 1990s and became 20 per cent in 2000. Moreover, the share of total FDI mainly comes into the manufacturing sector over the years. During the early 1970s, manufacturing sector accounted for 30 per cent of total inflows approximately. This has increased to about 45 per cent in the period of 1996-2000 though there was a mild decline in the later half of the 1990s mostly due to the currency crisis in the late 1997.

Table 7.2
Net Inflow of Foreign Direct Investment Classified by Sector (million USD and % share)

		1980-84	*1985-89*	*1990-94*	*1995-2000*	*2001-04*
1	Industry	266.53	1,582.58	2,494.11	7,355.63	3,660.20
		24.10	49.80	33.71	39.36	64.19
2	Food & sugar	29.21	149.42	166.24	548.17	132.17
		2.64	4.70	2.25	2.93	2.32
3	Textiles	8.81	112.13	185.51	337.63	68.62
		0.80	3.53	2.51	1.81	1.20
4	Metal & non metallic	14.47	157.84	308.30	1,023.24	517.71
		1.31	4.97	4.17	5.47	9.08

contd.

5	Electrical appliances	120.41	586.47	941.22	1,899.31	436.15
		10.89	18.45	12.72	10.16	7.65
6	Machinery & transport equipment	29.54	68.98	204.36	1,914.07	1,260.07
		2.67	2.17	2.76	10.24	22.10
7	Chemicals	30.55	183.01	502.71	751.30	468.69
		2.76	5.76	6.80	4.02	8.22
8	Petroleum products	12.04	1.08	-89.69	15.34	-120.43
		1.09	0.03	-1.21	0.08	-2.11
9	Construction materials	0.67	5.57	27.06	148.80	-34.38
		0.06	0.18	0.37	0.80	-0.60
10	Others	20.84	318.07	248.41	717.74	931.60
		1.88	10.01	3.36	3.84	16.34
11	Financial institutions	31.74	218.40	138.84	1,431.75	-830.42
		2.87	6.87	1.88	7.66	-14.56
12	Trade	164.75	471.24	1,339.01	4,359.79	367.68
		14.90	14.83	18.10	23.33	6.45
13	Construction	188.27	347.96	975.10	176.41	76.16
		17.02	10.95	13.18	0.94	1.34
14	Mining & quarrying	317.35	73.56	394.62	285.82	114.56
		28.69	2.31	5.33	1.53	2.01
15	Agriculture	13.64	45.84	38.14	17.44	3.71
		1.23	1.44	0.52	0.09	0.07
16	Services	95.70	150.85	265.81	1,732.90	658.51
		8.65	4.75	3.59	9.27	11.55
17	Investment	0.00	0.00	31.47	872.70	-538,70
		0.00	0.00	0.43	4.67	-9.45
18	Real estate	28.01	276.59	1,924.00	1,819.84	257.50
		2.53	8.70	26.01	9.74	4.52
19	Others	0.00	10.97	-203.10	637.98	1,933.12
		0.00	0.35	-2.75	3.41	33.90
20	Total	1,106.00	3,178.00	7,398.00	18,690.26	5,702.31
		100.00	100.00	100.00	100.00	100.00

Source: Bank of Thailand, unpublished data.

FDI FROM OECD COUNTRIES

It has already been explained that a significant proportion of FDI comes from OECD countries. The major receiving sector of OECD investment is industry whose share has increased from 52.7% in 1990 to 62.6% in 2000(Table 7.3). Figure 7.2 also shows the comparison of FDI from OECD and from other countries.

Figure 7.2
Comparison of total FDI and FDI flows from OECD Countries (million USD)

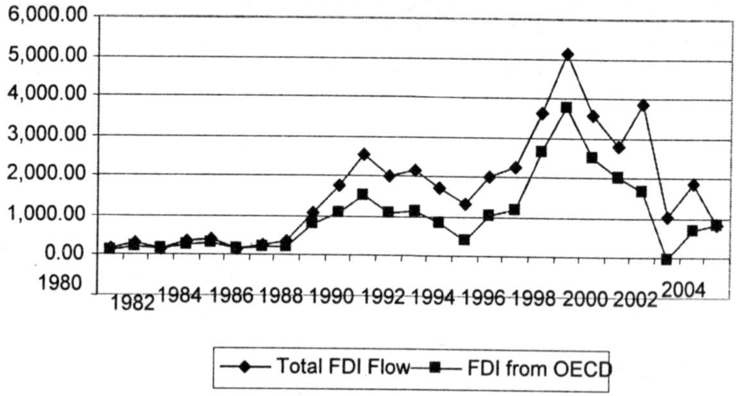

Table 7.3
Comparison of Total Inflow of FDI and OECD Inflow (million USD)

year	*Total net inflow of FDI*	*OECD net inflow of FDI*	*% Share of OECD inflow out of Total FDI inflow*
1980	189	108.83	57.58
1985	160	157.049	98.15
1990	2542	1535.20	60.39
1995	2003.9	1034.00	51.59
2000	2813.251	2019.94	71.80
2003	1882.127	696.92	37.02

Source: Bank of Thailand, published and unpublished data

Electrical and electronic appliances, petroleum products and chemicals have significant shares. As already discussed above that Japan was the major player in FDI in Thailand in the years prior to the crisis. Along with Japan, USA and the EU are also important sources of FDI. Japanese major investment was on electrical appliances, machinery and transport equipment throughout the 1990s. According to the data from Bank of Thailand, FDI inflows to Thailand and the pattern of FDI in different industries have changed over time. In the 1960s and 1970s, FDI was mostly channeled to import-substitution industries. In the 1980s, there were more FDI inflows in export-oriented industries. In the 1980-1989 periods, FDI inflows in electrical appliances and chemicals were significant. During the period of 1990-2000, industries receiving significant FDI inflows were chemicals, electrical appliances and machinery and transport equipment (Table 7.4). Transport equipment has become an important sector for FDI after 1995.

The Board of Investment (BOI) is the main agency to provide incentives to foreign investors. BOI promoted industries with a significant proportion of FDI including electronic and electrical products, chemicals, metals and machinery, and transport equipment.

Table 7.4
Share of Net Inflow of FDI from OECD among Sectors (%)

Sectors	*1987*	*1990*	*1995*	*2000*
1. Financial Institutions	8.70	5.62	0.34	7.96
2. Trade	17.26	16.12	23.13	10.91
3. Construction	12.68	6.47	1.94	0.77
4. Mining & Quarrying	3.08	1.62	2.87	0.15
5. Agriculture	2.86	1.45	0.74	0.02
6. Industry	45.94	52.72	58.64	62.64
6.1 Food	2.21	2.95	1.27	1.05
6.2 Textiles	4.97	1.75	3.46	0.65
6.3 Metal based and Non-metallic	9.83	6.41	5.95	6.27
6.4 Electrical appliances	11.80	20.78	24.12	16.22
6.5 Machinery & Transport Equip.	2.06	5.65	9.02	20.34
6.6 Chemicals	8.63	7.04	5.28	13.95
6.7 Petroleum products	0.01	2.43	5.32	0.01
6.8 Construction Materials	0.08	0.02	0.17	1.44
6.9 Other industry	6.35	5.68	4.05	2.70
7. Services	6.25	3.08	2.68	4.63
8. Investment	0.00	0.00	0.88	0.39
9. Real estate	3.22	11.81	8.78	1.33
10. Others	0.00	1.11	0.01	11.21
Total	100	100	100	100

Source: Computed by the author from the data (published and unpublished) of Bank of Thailand.

Thai exports of complex manufactured products are critically dependent on FDI. The fall in export growth has been larger in sectors dominated by domestic firms than in MNC dominated ones. This supports the widespread belief that restricted access to short-term finance is becoming a critical barrier to export growth, since domestic firms, particularly small ones, are more likely to suffer than MNCs.

It is widely believed that FDI promotes exports because large foreign companies that operate on a global scale enjoy significant economies of scale in marketing and possess a superior capability to access overseas markets. Foreign firms can also serve as a catalyst for domestic firms to increase their levels of exports (BOI statistics). FDI has played a very important role in Thailand's export performance.

FDI AND TECHNOLOGY

Thailand's industrial development has until the present time, relied much on FDI and the technology brought in by FDI companies. Although there are industries in which Thai citizens are major investors such as processed food, garments and jewelry, many technologically more sophisticated industries such as computer parts, electronics, and automotive industries are with substantial foreign investment, and also use, almost exclusively, imported technology.

There is no doubt that industrial development in Thailand has benefited much from FDI and technology transfer by foreign investors, if "technology transfer" is broadly defined to include the use of technology brought in by foreign companies. A study by the United Nations (ESCAP/UNCTAD, 1997), for example, categorized technology transfer into three channels: (a) through the delivery of technological, managerial and financial resources by foreign investing companies to the recipient enterprises; (b) through training and education, and purchase of capital equipment; and (c) through contractual agreements. Thailand has received technology transfer largely through the first channel.

There are several factors determining the extent of technology transfer. The first fact is the pattern of ownership and control. The study of ESCAP/UNCTC shows that technology transfer appears to be more extensive in the predominantly or wholly locally-owned companies. Technology transfer in transnational corporations is mostly capital-embodied, and peripheral or auxiliary technology, while the core technology has remained under foreign control. Most of these firms do not have an R&D department because they can import technology from their parent companies. By contrast, locally-owned companies which have local personnel in key management positions, tend to give opportunities to their local staff to be involved in R &D activities and in production activities.

The technology transfer process in joint ventures also varies with the strategies of different companies. If the investing foreign companies have the policy of keeping these firms as assembly lines, technology transfer will be limited to be technology necessary for operation and quality control for the product to meet accepted standard. By contrast, if the joint ventures have a policy to localize as many parts and components as possible, besides the upgrading of technology in the investment receiving company, some technology will also be transferred to the local supplies of the company, and contribute positively to local industrialization.

The second factor affecting the extent of technology transfer is the local absorptive capacity. The local absorptive capacity refers to both the availability of adequate facilities and human resources. Various studies (Kritayakirana, *et al.* 1989, Brimble and Sripaipan, 1994) conclude that Thai technology recipients have a low level of absorptive capacity because of limitations on human resources. R&D personnel, particularly engineers and scientists are in short supply and the available personnel usually lack knowledge, ability, work commitment and desirable attitude toward their jobs. Successful technology transfer is also affected by the inadequacy of necessary machinery and equipment and other facilities resulting from under investment in R&D related activities.

Regarding technology and skills in Thailand, it is found that although local firms were lagging behind foreign firms in terms of technology, they are more active in R&D activities. Most foreign companies have large R&D departments in their home countries and feel that it is not worthwhile to set up R&D units in Thailand. The performance of technology transfer though well in Thailand but it couldn't enjoy its full utilization because of the above mentioned factors.

THE POLICY REGIME OF FDI

Since around 1960, Thailand has put much emphasis on the promotion of private investment. In 1959, the Board of Investment (BOI) was established to administer the official investment promotion programme under the investment promotion law. The investment law was promulgated in 1960 and has been revised several times. In the 1960s, import-competing industries were emphasized. From around the mid-1970s the Thai government began to put more emphasis on export promotion policy and more incentives have been given to export industries since then. But it is not until the 1980s that FDI in export-oriented industries started to substantially come to invest in Thailand.

The incentives given to investment activities under promotion include tax exemption and reduction, including corporate income tax holidays ranging from 3 to 8 years, exemptions or reductions of duties and other taxes on machinery and raw material imports. In addition to tax incentives, the BOI has the discretionary power to prohibit imports, to raise tariff rates, or to impose import surcharge on products of the same type as those being produced by promoted firms. These restrictive trade measures, however, have not been frequently used. On the contrary, the policy of the Thai government in recent years has been towards trade liberalization. Tariff rates on imports have gradually been reduced in line with the World Trade Organization (WTO) and ASEAN Free Trade Area (AFTA) agreements. There is also an initiative to change the role of the BOI to emphasize less in granting tax incentives but more on investment promotion and facilitation.

Currently, the BOI's priority areas of investment promotion include basic industries, transportation system, public utilities, environmental protection and technological development. Export-oriented industries continue to be emphasized in investment promotion. Dispersion of industries to different geographical regions has also been stressed.

Since private investment was actively promoted, the Thai policy planners have put much importance to induce FDI. One of the objectives of BOI investment promotion was to attract FDI. Foreign investors could enjoy similar investment incentives to Thai investors. Some articles in the investment promotion law have in fact been written to ensure the confidence of foreign investors in investing in Thailand. Among these are a guarantee against nationalization of private business, permission for promoted foreign firms to own land and to bring in alien skilled workers in excess of those specified in other laws, and liberal terms set on the remittance of profits an other foreign exchange payments. The Thai government has also entered into agreements on the protection of investments and on the avoidance of double taxation with several major foreign investing countries, including Japan, the Untied States, and other countries in Europe and Asia.

At present, the office of the BOI has branches in major cities in different regions of the world, including Tokyo, Osaka, New York, Sydney and Frankfurt. In Thailand, the Office of the BOI offers investors a wide range of services. These include helping prospective investors of obtain permits required for conducing business, and gaining access to public utilities. A One-Stop Service Centre has been set up at the office of the BOI to help foreign investors obtain or renew their visas and work permits, and to facilitate the process of bringing in foreign skilled workers.

Although there exist some legislations that seem to restrict the freedom of foreign enterprises, in practice there has been virtually no control over the operations of foreign businesses in Thailand. The Alien Business Law (ABL) announced in 1972 specified that certain activities can only be undertaken by firms with a majority Thai ownership. The activities prescribed in the list of the ABL were mostly in agriculture, trade, services, and handicrafts, very few of which have substantial foreign capital participation. Although this ABL has virtually no effect in restricting FDI, in 1998 the Thai government has revoked the old ABL and replaced it with a law with more liberal terms on FDI with the purposes of ensuring prospective foreign investors that Thailand wants to welcome FDI and reduce all obstacles to restrict foreign operations in the country. According to the new Alien Business Law, a number of activities previously reserved to majority Thai-owned companies including those in brokerage services, wholesale and retailed trade and construction are now allowed a majority foreign ownership, and only a few activities relating to national security and culture are reserved for Thai nationals.

After the financial crisis, the BOI has provided some short-term measures to encourage new investment and the expansion of existing investment. For example, the incentives given to investment activities located in different locations have been modified. For investment projects in agricultural products which export at least 8-percent of their production, the BOI grants import duty exemption on machinery, regardless of location. For investment in supporting industries, an eight-year corporate income-tax exemption, and exemption of import duties on machinery are granted regardless of location. Foreigners may hold all or have a majority ownership share in these projects. Moreover, foreigners are allowed to have all or a majority of ownership shares in existing manufacturing projects. For export-oriented projects, the conditions governing the location of activities are mostly relaxed and export-oriented projects are allowed to import machinery with duty exemption in most cases. The conditions earlier set on local-content requirements in automobile and a few other industries have been abolished since January 2000.

Recently the BOI has revised its investment incentives to be more in line with WTO regulations. Currently, the BOI priority areas of investment promotion include investment projects in agricultural products, public utilities and infrastructure, environmental protection and conservation, and projects that involve technological and human resource development.

The investment policy regime in Thailand has been continually revised to reflect the broad development of the economy and its trade regime from the era of import substitution to export promotion, and from pre-crisis industrial boom to post-crisis liberalization. Domestic laws and regulations were promulgated or amended to facilitate FDI since the early seventies when Thailand adopted the export promotion strategy to stimulate domestic growth. As a result, investment policy has become increasingly liberal during the past three decades as the country embarked on the path of industrialization.

The Thai FDI regime is one that concentrates mainly on the provision of fiscal incentives, in particular, taxes and duties exemptions. A salient feature of the regime is that, unlike many Asian countries, the government does not have specific industries or sectors that it selectively promotes. There is, however, a general indication that the high-technology investment projects that would help promote the upgrading of the Thai industries are given priority and thus, are likely to receive promotional incentives or be allowed to operate in businesses normally reserved for national commercial entities. Another important feature of the regime is its emphasis on most-favoured nation (MFN) and non-discrimination. All foreign investors are eligible for similar rights and subject to similar obligations under the domestic laws, while local and foreign investors are eligible for the same tax and non-tax incentives offered by local investment promotion agencies.

THE LEGAL FRAMEWORK

The FDI regime in Thailand is shaped by three main laws, the Foreign Business Act of 1999, the Investment Promotion Act of 1977 and the Industrial Estate Authority of Thailand Act of 1979.

The Investment Promotion Act 1977

The Investment Promotion Act sets out principles and procedures for investment promotion, including protection guarantees, tax and non-tax incentives offered to foreigners. The act established the Board of Investment (BOI) as the principal agency responsible for promoting investment through the granting of investment incentives and guarantees. Since its promulgation in 1977, it has gone through several amendments in keeping with changes in the government economic policy.

The act empowers the BOI to grant various fiscal and non-fiscal incentives for foreign and domestic investment that meet national economic development. These incentives and privileges currently include exemption from or a reduction in import duties on imported machinery, materials, and components; exemption from corporate income tax for 3–8 years, with permission to carry losses forward; and exemption from dividend tax during corporate income tax holidays. Foreign firms may also (a) receive permission to bring in foreign technicians and experts to work on a promoted project; (b) own land in connection with a promoted project for business offices and living residences. The Investment Promotion Act also contains provisions that guarantee investors against adverse shifts in government policies, rules, and regulations (such as price controls or export restrictions), as well as competition from state enterprises and other government agencies, except those already in operation.

The Industrial Estate Authority of Thailand Act 1979

To promote the de-concentration of industry away from the Bangkok area, the Industrial Estate Authority of Thailand Act 1979 provides special incentives for investors locating in industrial estates situated in regional areas. These industrial estates comprise both general industrial zones and export-processing zones.

Incentives offered by the Industrial Estate Authority are similar to those offered by the Board of Investment. The only difference is that the investment privileges are available to investment projects that are located in the industrial estates. These include the right to own land in an industrial estate, permission to obtain work permits for foreign technicians and experts, and the right to remit foreign currency abroad. Businesses operating in an export processing zone are entitled to additional incentives and privileges such as exemptions from special fees, import and export duty, value-added tax, and excise tax applied on exports and imported machinery, equipment, and tools used in the manufacture of goods and in the construction of factories or buildings taxes or goods destined for another export-processing zone.

ROLE OF INTERNATIONAL DEVELOPMENT AGENCIES IN FDI

The role of international development agencies in FDI in Thailand is minimal. This is because Thailand has already graduated from the list of countries that are in need of financial assistance from international development agencies, like Asian Development Bank or the World Bank.

Multilateral agreement

The TRIMs Agreement negotiated during the Uruguay Round of the GATT aimed to discipline investment policies that are inconsistent with Article III.4 (on national treatment) and Article XI.1 (on quantitative restrictions) of the GATT; that is, it deals with the investment dimension of the GATT trade agreement. The TRIMs Agreement obliges all WTO member countries to phase out local content and export performance requirements imposed on foreign firms. The TRIMs Agreement was instrumental in achieving investment policy reform in Thailand. To comply with the agreement, Thailand gradually abolished its trade-related investment measures. New projects approved to receive investment incentives after April 1993 were no longer subject to local content requirements, except in the dairy product and vehicle assembly industries. Local content requirements for vehicle assembly were eliminated in 1999, with local content requirements for dairy products to be phased out by the end of 2003. Export performance requirements were lifted in August 2000.

Regional agreements

As member of the Asia Pacific Economic Cooperation (APEC) and Association of Southeast Asian Nations (ASEAN), Thailand observes the non-binding investment principles of the Asia Pacific Economic Cooperation (APEC) forum, and the binding ASEAN Investment Area.

As we have already seen that the type of industries catering FDI has changed quite a bit and so also the share of countries thus this will have a definite impact on the environment.

ENVIRONMENTAL IMPACT OF FDI

Environmental Concerns

Indeed, most of the countries seek to attract FDI. In competing for limited foreign capital, host countries may be tempted to lower their environmental standards in order to increase the relative attractiveness of the location to multinational companies. This "race to the bottom" allow multinational companies to take advantage of weak environmental laws in host countries.

Most bilateral investment treaties (BITs) do not address environmental concerns. As for the case of FTAs, the draft Thai-US FTA, which is based on the Singapore-US FTA, does contain a specific provision on environment. It states that "nothing in the agreement in the investment chapter shall prevent parties from adopting, maintaining, or enforcing any measures that are of environmental concern". The provision serves to ensure that—in the process of protecting the rights of foreign investors, the sovereign regulatory space on environmental issues are preserved. That is, should the host government undertake environmental policies or measures that adversely affected foreign companies, the latter will not be able to file for arbitral awards.

It is interesting to note that none of the mentioned bilateral and regional agreement addresses corporate responsibilities or code of conduct beyond what is stipulated by the host country's law, which tends to be weak in terms of both the legal provisions and its enforcement.

Thailand has had its share of environmental problems associated with MNCs. In most developing countries, when it comes to government policies, private commercial interests often supercede those of the public such as environment, health, safety and livelihood. This is often the case when money and politics are deeply entangled and when there is no effective check-and-balance within the political machinery.

As stated earlier that, the contribution of FDI to the expansion of the manufacturing sector may intensify pollution problems. The effect of FDI on the environment has not been studied thoroughly in Thailand. The literature primarily concentrates on the role of FDI on Thailand's economy. However, Puppavesa and Pungasri (1990) have attempted in their work on the impact of FDI on air, water and hazardous waste. It shows that non-metal products industry is the largest polluter followed by the food and textile industries. The study concludes that FDI does not seriously contribute (accounted for only about 16 percent of the total FDI), directly or indirectly, to the problem of air pollution according to the survey of 1990. Further FDI again does not seriously add to the problem of SPM emissions in Thailand. The study has also found that FDI does not significantly contribute to the problem of hazardous waste generation. By 1989, only a small portion of promoted foreign firms concentrated in the basic metal industry. Again the BOI data illustrate quite clearly that the relative concentration of FDI is highest in the rank 2 (includes industries with the potential to generate moderate amounts of waste with low levels of contamination) industries. This concentration of FDI indicates that there is potential for FDI to generate moderate amounts of hazardous waste with low levels of contamination. Japanese investment does not concentrate in the rank industries more than those of other countries. However, in magnitude of investment, Japanese investment has potential to produce more hazardous waste than other countries.

Thus the findings of Puppavesa & Pungsari have revealed that the impact of FDI on the environment has not been severe before the 1990s though waste related pollution and especially the Japan's contribution in this respect raises some worriness.

Our study has considered the period after the 1990s. For this analysis the current study extended the model developed in Chapter 4. The study attempts to examine the implication of the FDI on the environment using Input-Output model for the year 2000.

Let us recollect the equations 16 and 17 of Chapter 4. Using equations we have calculated the pollution content of FDI in Thailand from rest of the world (589.59 KtC, 4.95 KtS and 5.27 for CO_2, SO_2 and NOx respectively) as well as OECD (428.49 KtC, 3.54 KtS and 4.07 for CO_2, SO2 and NOx respectively) in the year 2000.

Equation 4* and 4** (Chapter 4) has further been used to compute the pollution content of export induced by FDI. Results for FDI from the rest of the world and OECD are found to be 326.50 KtC and 343.14 KtC for CO_2, 3.38 KtS and 3.09 KtS for SO_2 and 3.51 and 3.06 for NOx respectively. These values indicate the contribution of FDI to the generation of pollution from the export sectors.

As is the case for trade, the environmental effects of FDI can be positive or negative (UN 1995). FDI helped spur relatively Thailand's competitiveness in international trade. The increase in competition for goods has prompted investors from high cost production countries to relocate their production to low cost countries. This has happened in Thailand. There has been migration of dirty industries to Thailand from the developed countries like Japan.

Our earlier analysis has clearly indicated that there has been a considerable change in the composition of exports from agro based to manufacturing over the period 1980 to 2000. And FDI has played an important role in this shift. The shift in the composition of FDI from domestic-market oriented production to export oriented manufacturing production in Thailand has closely mirrored the shift in the domestic trade policy regime (Kohpaiboon, 2003). More recently, assembly activities in electronics and electrical goods industries have been the main attraction to foreign investors. Thus the above discussion shows that the environmental implication of FDI in Thailand has not been positive.

While analyzing the effects of trade policies and export expansion on the domestic environment Jha et al.(1999) stated that the Thai domestic and foreign investment promotion had mixed effects on the environment and conclude that "because of the various influences of export promotion are does not appear to be any systematic effect of FDI on the environment". However, this chapter makes a quantitative assessment of FDI on the environment and tends to conclude that the impact has not been friendly.

8

Conclusion and Policy Options

To promote liberal trade while maintaining and strengthening protection of the environment and natural resources is one of the major policy challenges of the decade. International trade contributes to economic growth, benefits all participating countries, while growth, in turn, increases the demand for environmental quality and provides the financial resource for environmental protection. It is commonly assumed by economists and environmentalists alike that greater economic openness will lead to increase pollution in developing countries, as free trade will increase environmental degradation in developing countries. Thus there are points at which trade and environmental objectives are in potential conflict. If left unattended, these conflicts can weaken the trade system and become an obstacle to sustainable development. In the last 20 years, environmental distribution issues gained increasing attention in the international debate in particular since the recognition of sustainable development as the guiding principle for future global development (WCED, 1987).

Thus the impact of trade liberalisation on the environment is a matter of debate. Two conflicting hypotheses have emerged from the debate. First one is pollution haven hypothesis (PHH). This hypothesis suggests that the developed countries impose tougher environmental policies than do the developing countries, which results in distortion of existing patterns of comparative advantage. So the polluting industries shift operations from the developed to the developing countries; developing countries thus become "pollution havens." The second hypothesis, the factor endowment hypothesis (FEH), states that trade liberalisation will result in trade patterns consistent with the Heckscher-Ohlin-Vanek (HOV) theory of comparative advantage based on factor endowment differentials. Rich countries are typically well endowed with capital. Since capital-intensive goods are often also pollution-intensive, factor-endowment theories of international trade predict that rich countries specialize in polluting goods. Thus the manifestation of the PHH is in direct conflict with the FEH. This debate is of great concern among economists, environmentalists and world bodies like WTO.

Thailand is a good laboratory for testing these two hypotheses. Among all south and south East Asian countries Thailand can be regarded as one of the fastest growing economy. The average annual growth rate between 1980 and 2004 is approximately 7 percent. The most prosperous time of the Thai economy was during 1986-96, the period of highest economic growth averaging 9.1 percent per annum. This high growth was led by the growth in the manufacturing sector. Liberalised trade policy has been the main driver and corner stone of this growth of the Thai economy.

The Thai exports have also increased significantly during 1980 to 2004. With the rapid growth of Thailand's trade over the past 15 years, the composition of Thailand's exports has changed significantly. In 1985, 53% of the values of Thailand's exports comprising agricultural & agro based industrial products but it came down to 8% by the year 2000. On the other hand 80% of the value of exports came from manufacturing and services. The most dominating sectors are electronics sector, particularly computers, computer modules and integrated circuits with the increasing world demand.

Imports have also experienced a similar growth like exports in Thailand. Imports mainly provide the raw materials and equipment necessary to fuel the rapidly developing exports of the manufacturing sector.

Since the present study is also focusing Thailand's trade with OECD separately, a discussion on the trade pattern of the two is needed to have a better view.

OECD is a major trading partner of Thailand holding a share of 55% since 1980s. But the pattern of trade has changed from OECD trade surplus in 1995 to a significant Thai trade surplus in 2000. This surplus accounted for 72% of Thailand's overall trade surplus and has significantly helped to strengthen Thailand's external accounts and the external value of the baht. The intra industry trade always become a feature of the Thai trade history which is more prominent in case of OECD. The main Thai exports to OECD and imports include machinery, electrical items and parts, electronics and motor vehicles. OECD's share (more than 65% in 2000) was the most important source of foreign direct investment in Thailand.

Further the trade performance of Thailand has changed considerably which is reflected in the sector of production and consumption. In the later half of the 1990s the situation started changing towards more capital intensive industry from labour intensive because of shifting of the exports towards more emerging industries. This diversification of exports was successfully supported and encouraged by the investment promotion activities of the Board of Investment (BOI), Thailand which attracted foreign capital to few selected export sectors.

The intense economic and largely industrial development, significant changes in trade pattern and the production technology have important implications for the environment and also serious consequences for the future of the Thai economy.

With this in mind the current study has examined the impact of trade liberalisation on the environment in Thailand during the period 1980-2000. It attempts to contribute on recent debate on trade and environment focusing on two contradictory hypotheses i.e. pollution haven and factor endowments for Thailand and the rest of the world and also for the OECD exclusively. The environmental indicators for this study concentrate only on CO_2, SO_2 and NOx emissions from fossil fuel combustion. The study measures Thailand's environmental gains or losses from trade with other countries. The pollution terms of trade index has been used to test the pollution haven hypothesis for the current study while the labour requirement and capital requirement of Thailand's export and import have been computed to test the so called factor abundance hypothesis. Further it analyses the implications of FDI on the environment.

Chapter 1 presents a brief introduction based on the theoretical understanding of the recent trade and environment issue. It also discusses various impacts of trade on the environment followed by some description on the trade and environment measures playing in the international platform.

Chapter 2 reviews the growing literature on trade and environment (Tobey, 1990; Lucas, et al.1992; Low and Yeates, 1992; Mani and Wheeler, 1998; Cole and Elliot 2001; Xing and Kolstad, 2002; Eskeland & Harrison, 2003; Copeland and Taylor, 2003; Smarzynska and Wei, 2004; Waldkirch and Gopinath, 2004). Several attempts have used Input-Output model to address the issue (Wyckoff and Roop 1994; Gale and Lewis 1995; Antweiler 1996;

Proops et al. 1999; Machado et al. 2001; Munksgaard and Pedersen 2001; Wadeskog 2002). But only a few have addressed the PHH and FEH using Input-Output model (Mukhopadhyay 2004; Mukhopadhyay & Chakraborty, 2005 a, b).

From the brief literature it is revealed that the debate on trade and its impact on the environment is still open. The methodologies employed to test the hypotheses are widely varied so are the results. Discussions on Thailand's trade-environmental relation received attention in recent years (TDRI 1996, 2000; Jha et al.1999; TEI 2000). Unfortunately, no comprehensive work has been done on Thailand involving these issues together, in particular using I-O techniques. So the current study concerns with this.

Chapter 3 presents an overview of the Thai economy including the growth of the economy, industrial and trade policies. It also focuses on environmental problems and policies.

Chapter 4 presents the methodology of the current research. It is based on Leontief's Input-Output framework (Leontief, 1951). This is a method of systematically quantifying the mutual interrelationships among the various sectors of a complex economic system. Methodology has been suitably modified and extended for the work.

Three models have been formulated. Model 1 estimates the pollution haven effect assuming HOV i.e. of identical technology (Thailand's trade with the ROW and OECD). Again the same model has been applied by relaxing the H-O-V (in case of Thailand's trade with OECD). To derive the pollution embodied in imports the study considers the emission intensities of USA instead of Thailand. Here USA has been considered as a representative of OECD. Model 2 explicates the factor endowment hypothesis for Thailand's trade with the ROW and OECD. Model 3 finally studies the impact of FDI on the environment. Various sources used in the experiment of the model are reported in Chapter 4.

Chapter 5, 6 and 7 present the findings of the work. Chapter 5 and 6 stress on two aspects i.e. why pollution haven matters for Thailand and why factor endowment hypothesis does not. The results clearly ensure that Thailand moves to pollution haven in 2000 for all the cases—rest of the world and OECD. To define the pollution haven effect the study considered PTOT as an indicator.

During the 1980s and 1990s the values of PTOT were below 100. This implies that Thailand export goods that are more environment friendly than goods it imports. But the situation has become changed during 2000. For the case of ROW the indices is quite high during 2000 for all the three pollutants. Thailand's export is 35% more pollution intensive for CO_2. SO_2's performance is almost similar with a marginal higher value. In case of NOx the figure is little less than the other two pollutants but it stands above 100(25% more pollution intensive exports). In case of OECD also the values of PTOT for 2000 are above 100 for all the three pollutants. The result supports the pollution haven hypothesis in 2000. The result of PTOT in case of other attempt (extension of model 1 relaxing the H-O assumption) also reveals a similar trend but the values are really higher than the values of PTOT in H-O assumption case in model 1. The values of PTOT are 2.25, 2.79 and 1.41 for CO_2, SO_2 and NOx respectively. It clearly ensures wide differences of technology and emission intensities between Thailand and OECD (USA as a representative of OECD). The improved technology and lower emission intensities are responsible for the higher values of PTOT in the extended model. On the whole Thailand is supporting pollution haven hypothesis or at least not to contradict in 2000.

On the other hand evidence from Chapter 6 is not in conformity with factor endowment hypothesis in 2000. The study has offered several explanations for these conflicting findings.

It has been observed that composition of export has changed during 1980 to 2000 from agro based export commodity to manufacturing base leading to emerging group of the manufacturing sector. The structure of Thailand's exports in the 1990s has diversified into a wide variety of products. Agriculture's contribution to GDP came down so also exports. This rapid decline in agriculture was partly as a result of falling prices, faltering world trade and competitors in world rice market.

These facts have also influenced the production technology of the economy. Since the country is switching from agro based to core manufacturing further landing on emerging sectors, changes in technology from labour intensive to capital intensive is highly expected in this regard. It has also been compounded by shortage of skilled manpower (discussed in Chapter 6).

The major reason for this shift in the composition of exports and the production technology has been made possible due to a significant change in the trade policy of the economy. Import substitution was the main objective of the Thai trade history since the 1970s to promote industrialization. The use of tariff was the major instrument to influence the country's development path and it effectively began in 1974 to promote domestic industry. The export promotion policy was more effective in the late 1980s. The average import tariffs have declined significantly from 30.24 per cent in 1990 to 21 per cent in 1995 and then 17.01 per cent in 1997. Further the most important policy of Thailand and the EU under the *Asia-Europe Investment Promotion Action Plan* aims to promote public and private sector co-operation on the issue of removing trade and investment barriers between the two regions.

Coupled with the above mentioned trade strategies and policies relating to trade liberalization weak and non-compliance of environmental regulation has also responsible for pollution haven effect. Though Thailand had passed several acts and laws since 1975 but the monitoring and enforcement was very weak. Moreover, Environmental standards are always far below than the standards set by OECD and other East Asian NIES. These facts have further been helpful for the migration of dirty industries to Thailand.

The study has also attempted to compute the pollution content of FDI and also FDI from the OECD countries (Chapter 7). The results show that the pollution contents are 589.59 KtC and 428.49 KtC for $CO_{2,}$ 4.95 KtS and 3.54 KtS for SO2 and 5.27 and 4.07 for NOx respectively. Moreover the foreign direct investment can be treated as an input in the economy to enhance its productive capacity. This in turn has influenced the export performance of the economy and generated pollution. The pollution content of exports induced by FDI are found to be 326.50 KtC and 343.14 KtC for CO_2, 3.38 KtS and 3.09 KtS for SO2 and 3.51 and 3.06 for NOx respectively. These values clearly indicate the contribution of FDI to the generation of pollution from the export sectors.

Results show that the predictions of the pollution haven hypothesis are strong when factor abundance motives for trade are weak. Since the pollution haven and factor endowments hypotheses offer such different predictions, we have designed our empirical work to facilitate a weighing of their relative strength. Thailand loses from trade in terms of emissions in the year 2000. Further the analysis of the implication of FDI on the environment has not been environment friendly. Our results in this regard are thought provocative.

Not surprisingly we have demonstrated that the country, Thailand with weaker environmental policy and non-compliance of environmental regulations exports dirty goods. However the result relies on the absence of production externalities. Brander and Taylor (1997) have argued that this result can be overturned if lax environmental policy leads to resource depletion in the long run. If the two countries (for example, Thailand and OECD) differ only in their per capita income then the richer country will have more stringent pollution standards. Trade will therefore create a pollution haven in the poor country. Free trade leads LDCs to change the composition of its output toward specialization in dirty good production (Copeland and Taylor, 2003).

The current findings can be compared with those of other studies. Results are in tune with those of Low and Yeats (1992) and Waldkirch and Gopinath (2004) but contradict Busse(2004) and Mukhopadhay & Chakraborty (2005). On the other hand Mani and Wheeler (1999), Cole and Eliott(2001), Copeland and Taylor(2003) provide mixed results. On the whole our study provides stronger evidence on the two hypotheses. In respect of FDI's implication on the environment, Thailand's experience as evident from the current study is in sharp contrast with that of Singapore, one of the major destinations for FDI in Asia since 1991 which has acquired international reputation for stringent environmental standards and apparently has had no difficulty in attracting foreign investment.

Over the past two decades, in an effort to combat rising levels of pollution, most Asian nations have introduced pollution control systems similar to those in developed countries. However, ongoing enforcement challenges coupled with the need for a better understanding of pollution control mechanisms, within the Asian context, have promoted the requirement for more effective pollution control policies especially to promote exports while protecting the environment. Singapore and other NIES have gathered better results in this regard.

Singapore's approach is on building and sustaining a pragmatic, tough, competent, and fair command-and control environmental agency, the ENV (Ministry of Environment). The pragmatic and tougher emissions standards were complemented by strong programs to monitor ambient air and water quality. To this end, the ENV added a rigorous, honest and fair inspection and enforcement program (Rock, 2002).

By the early 1990s ambient air and water quality in Singapore was equal to that in the countries that belong to the Organisation for Economic Co-operation and Development (OECD).

The current study has also important implications for other developing countries of the region. For example, Malaysia, the Philippines and China which are also following a similar export driven growth path induced by FDI would likely to have the similar type of impacts on the environment. These countries of course have stricter environmental regulations compared to those of Thailand, however far below OECD standards. FDI as a percentage of GDP is around 3-4% in these countries (Krishnakumar, 2005). So the possibility of being pollution havens cannot be ruled out for these countries. However, it requires thorough investigation.

POLICY OPTIONS

In an effort to control and reduce pollution, Thailand has adopted a "command and control" (CAC) approach, based on the European and American pollution control models, which relies on laws and regulations that establish emission limits, and the subsequent enforcement of these laws.

However, the CAC approach has had limited success, primarily due to the stringent environmental standards that are beyond the capacity of certain industrial sectors of Thailand. This situation is further worsened by a general lack of competent monitoring and enforcement measures, resulting from insufficient human resources and a lack of training within the government sector (as discussed in Chapter 5).

Stricter environmental measures tend to serve both the interests of the preservation of the nation's natural resources, and the promotion of its long-term economic interests. The question is then, which measures will be successful and how can they be effectively promoted and implemented?

In order to control pollution, Thailand must also enact adequate pollution standards. While many standards are at or above international levels, current acceptable ambient standards for air pollution levels and for many pollutant emission levels are, for instance, not up to accepted international standards, and often are poorer than even regional averages. If Thailand is to make a serious attempt to control damage due to air pollution, it needs to re-evaluate environmental quality standards, taking internationally accepted scientific information into consideration.

The first step is to ensure that companies are informed of the relevant environmental standards and options. Many businesses are simply unaware of either the regulations governing their production and/or methods for reducing resource consumption and pollution. Towards this end, both the public and private sectors should work towards creating information networks and clearing-houses, through which companies can find out about regulation, technology, and alternative production methods relevant to their needs. These information networks could serve to showcase the potential economic, as well as environmental benefits of new technologies, for instance. If companies are made aware of such resources, they themselves will choose to upgrade their current practices. Attempts in this direction, being made by local

NGOs and pro-business organizations should continue to be developed and to be enhanced to reach smaller scale firms.

An even bigger obstacle than lack of information is a lack of financial resources. Obviously, providing more money for technology acquisition and for enforcement of environmental regulation will be helpful.

A measure which has the potential to promote both trade and increased compliance with environmental regulation is the promotion of special investment zones in combination with pollution control zones. Concentrating businesses in certain areas also makes easier the task of monitoring environmental compliance. Moreover, basic monitoring of business' compliance must exist.

Similarly taxes on environmental technology should be reduced so as not to penalize prospective buyers. The Thai government has already taken steps in this direction, such as reducing import duties on machinery designed to solve specific environmental problems. However, businesses complain that the red-tape involved in attaining these benefits is too complicated. For example, many claim that the requirement of proof that the given product be used exclusively for environmental protection purposes is too restrictive, since many technologies and products are multipurpose. Perhaps more useful would be an alternative criteria which requires a product simply to demonstrate significant environmental benefits.

Given the above framework of broad policy suggestions we now recommend a few specific measures involving trade and environment.

(a) Instead of too much emphasis on the exports of capital intensive goods, a balanced export strategy combining labour and capital intensive goods can be thought of.

To achieve this Government should enhance the international competitiveness of Thai exports by reducing production costs, for example, restructuring import tariffs, overhauling customs procedures, and seeking to expand into new markets.

In this context, human resource development should continue to build up the supply of skilled labour needed for new and advanced technologies.

(b) To maintain environmental quality the trade restricting measures for pollution intensive export goods should be adopted.

(i) The Thai government may consider implementing taxes or tariffs based on the environmental impact of the production of the goods, known as *eco-duties.*

(ii) A tax on fuel would be the appropriate measure to motivate the adoption of fuel efficient production techniques.

(iii) A tax on the most pollutive inputs (e.g. a tax on high-sulfur fuel), or conversely tax reductions for pollution reducing practices (e.g. for switching from fossil fuels to natural gas).

The government also needs to discourage highly pollutive industries, and remove subsidies from products and practices which do not meet strict environmental standards or for which more environmentally friendly alternatives have been found. Instead of subsidizing pesticides, for instance, the same revenue could be dedicated to promoting integrated pest-management (IPM) methods. Such a practice has already been implemented successfully elsewhere in the region.

(iv) A tax on emissions is another suitable policy instruments to motivate the adoption of abatement technologies.

(v) Since the command and control regulatory policies are often difficult to enforce the use of economic instrument (for example, fuel user charge, emission charge, and pollution management fee) might be more effective and less expensive which would make greener policies more attractive to businesses.

(vi) Another option may include using market instruments such as tradable pollution permits to ensure compliance. Such an alternative has several attractive features. It would not only help to bring pollution down to controlled levels, but would also provide an incentive for the polluters to monitor one another, thus lessening the burden on government authorities, and provide an additional source of income for government environmental programs.

(c) The technological improvement in producing green products would require more R&D expenditure. To encourage that government can provide financial incentives in the form of tax rebate/exemption to the firms. In this context the government can also think of providing subsidies to the users of imported technology necessary for the production of green product. Greener trade should be given continuous preference by the Thai government.

(d) To contribute towards sustainable development and a higher quality of life, both the government and the industrial sector need to take actions to reduce and eliminate the currently unsustainable practices used in production processes and the management of industrial wastes. Possible solutions include:

(i) Increased enforcement is necessary to make the current laws effective for controlling pollution.

(ii) The public can play a role in pollution prevention using public pressure on polluters and regulatory agencies through the relatively free Thai press.

(e) Last but not least concerning foreign environmental regulation affecting Thai producers, the Thai government should adopt more proactive stance. Stricter standards are in the offing. So an early action of the Thai government would be helpful to the Thai firms to adjust to external regulations.

Thus the study suggests that the Thai government should integrate both trade environmental policies in a coherent manner (trade related environmental policies, TREMS and environment related trade measures, ERTM) to achieve the objectives of gains from trade while protecting environment.

DIRECTIONS FOR FUTURE RESEARCH

The present study has made a modest effort to address the issue of trade and the environment focusing on Thailand. The work is not comprehensive as it has considered selected indicators of air pollution only (CO_2, SO_2 NOx). We know that there are several other critical environmental indicators such as water pollution, solid and hazardous waste. To have a comprehensive picture of the environmental impact of trade these indicators need to be included in the analysis. Like air, waste water is also a serious problem in Thailand. In addition recently the hazardous waste generated from electrical and electronic appliances receives importance due to the international regulations like WEEE[1] (come into force from 1st July 2006) and RoHS[1] directives. As we have seen from our study that Thailand is exporting electrical and electronic appliances after the mid 1990s because of increased demand in the international market, a study is necessary to assess the implications of these external regulation (UNCTAD, 2006).

Chapter 7 of the current study has made a very preliminary assessment of the impact of FDI on the environment. Unfortunately no thorough research has been carried out in Thailand on this challenging issue. Future research demands a detailed evaluation.

Since Thailand has already ratified the Kyoto protocol, in this respect the impact of trade on climate change will be another possible area of research.

NOTE

1. The Restriction of certain Hazardous Substances (RoHS) and the Waste Electrical and Electronic Equipment (WEEE) Directives are complex pieces of environmental legislation, which will affect each and every electronics manufacturer directly or indirectly, regardless of geographical location or the equipment produced.

   The WEEE Directive aims to reduce the waste arising from electrical and electronic equipment; and improve the environmental performance of all those involved in the life cycle of electrical and electronic products like manufacturing, selling, distributing, recycling or treating electrical and electronic equipment (household appliances, IT and telecommunications equipment, audiovisual and lighting equipment, electrical and electronic tools, toys, leisure and sports equipment, medical devices and automatic dispensers). The Directive covers WEEE used by consumers and for professional purposes. The RoHS Regulations implement the provisions of the European Parliament and Council Directive on the Restrictions of the Use of Certain Hazardous Substances in Electrical and Electronic Equipment (2002/95/EC) in order to protect human health and the environment by restricting the use of certain hazardous substances in new equipment; and complement the Waste Electrical and Electronic Equipment (WEEE) Directive (2002/96/EC). The RoHS Directive covers the same categories as the WEEE Directive, with the exception of medical devices and monitoring and control instruments.

Bibliography

Abbott, P. C. and S. L. Haley (1988), "International Trade Theory and Natural Resource Concepts", in Sutton, J. D. (eds.), Agricultural Trade and Natural Resources: Discovering the Critical Linkages, Lynne Rienner Publishers, Inc., Boulder &London.

Ahmed, N. (2002), 'Environmental Spillovers—Energy Use and Carbon Leakages in the OECD', *Paper presented at the International Input-Output Conference* held at Montreal, Canada, October 2002.

Almon, C. and A. Ruiz-Moncago (1991), Simulation of a Mexico-USA Free Trade Agreement, *Economic Systems Research*, 3(1): 93-98.

Antweiler, W (1996), The Pollution Terms of Trade, *Economic Systems Research*, 8(4): 361-5.

Antweiler, W., B. R. Copeland, and M. S. Taylor (1998), Is Free Trade Good for the Environment? *NBER Working Paper No. W6707*, August.

Antweiler, W., B. R. Copeland, and M. S. Taylor (2001), Is Free Trade Good for the Environment?, *American Economic Review*, 91(4): 877-908, September.

APFEED (2002), 'World Trade and Environment' in *Towards a New Decade of Trade and Environment*, Thailand Environment Institute and Department of Industrial Works, Thailand.

Audley, J. J. (1997), "Green Politics and Global Trade", Washington, D. C.: Georgetown University Press.

Ayres, R. U. and A. V. Kneese (1969), Production, Consumption, and Externalities, *American Economic Review* 59(3): 282-297.

Azevedo, M. P. (1982), "Trade in Hazardous Substances: An Examination of US Regulation," in S. Rubin, ed., *Environment and Trade*. New Jersey: Allanheld, Osmun and Co.

Balasubramanyam, V.N., M.A. Salisu, and D. Sapsford. (1996), Foreign Direct Investment and Growth in EP and IS Countries, *Economic Journal*, 106 (434): 92-105.

Bank of Thailand, Quarterly Bulletin (Various Issues).

——,Annual Report (Various Issues).

Bank of Thailand(1998), Annual Report.

Bank of Thailand, Thailand's Key Economic Indicators, Macro Economics Data Section.

Bank of Thailand, Export Classified by Product Group, Macro Economics Data Section.

Bank of Thailand, Net inflow of Foreign Direct Investment, Unpublished Data.

Bartik, T. J. (1988), The Effects of Environmental Regulation on Business Location in the United States. *Growth and Change* 19 (3): 22–44.

Baumol, W. J. (1971), "Environmental Protection, International Spillovers and Trade", Wicksell Lecture, Stockholm: Almquist and Wicksell.

Baumol, W., and W.E. Oates (1975), "The Theory of Environmental Policy", New Jersey: Prentice-Hall.

Baumol, W., and W.E. Oates (1988), "The Theory of Environmental Policy", Second edition, New York: Cambridge University Press.

Bhagwati, J. (1971), "The Generalized Theory of Distortions and Welfare", in Bhagwati, J. et al. Eds., *Trade, Balance of Payments and Growth*, Papers in International Economics in Honor of Charles P. Kindleberger, Amsterdam: North-Holland Publishing Compang, 69-90.

Bhagwati, J. (1973) "The Theory of Immiserizing Growth; Further Applications" in M. Connolly and A. Swoboda (eds.),

International Trade and Money, University of Toronto Press, Toronto: 45-54.

Bhagwati, J. (1978), "Anatomy and Consequences of Exchange Control Regimes", Balinger Publishing, New York.

Bhagwati, J. (1985), "Investing Abroad: Esmée Fairbairn Lecture", Lancaster University Press, Lancaster.

Bhagwati, J. (1994), Free Trade: Old and New Challenges, *Economic Journal*, 104 (423): 231-246.

Bhagwati, J. (1993a), The Case for Free Trade, *Scientific American* 269: 42-49.

Bhagwati, J. (1993b), "Trade and the Environment: The False Conflict?" Zaelke, D.P. Orbuch and R. F. Housman (eds.), *Trade and the Environment: Law, Economics and Policy*, Washingten, DC: Island Press.

Bhagwati, J. and H. T. Patrick (1990), "Aggressive Unilateralism: America's 301, Trade Policy and the World Trading System", Ann Arbor: University of Michigan Press.

Blizer, C. R., R. S. Eckaus, S. Lahiri and A. Meeraus (1990), "A General Equilibrium Analysis of Carbon Emission Restrictions on Economic Growth in a Developing Country", Paper presented at a Workshop on Economic /Energy / Environmental Modeling for Climate Policy Analysis, the World Bank, Washington, D. C., October.

Borensztein, E., J.D. Gregorio, and J.W. Lee, (1998), How Does Foreign Direct Investment Affect Economic Growth? *Journal of International Economics*, 45:115-35.

Brander, J. and S. Taylor (1997), International Trade between Consumer and Conservationist Countries, *Resource and Energy Economics* 19(4): 267-297.

Bowen, H. (1983), Changes in the International Distribution of Resources and Their Impact on US Comparative Advantage, *Review of Economics and Statistics*, 65: 402-414.

Brecher, R. A. and E. E. Choudhri (1988), "The Factor Content of Consumption in Canada and the United States: A Two-Country Test of the Heckscher-Ohlin-Vanek Model", Feenstra, R. C. (ed). *Empirical Methods for International Trade*, Cambridge: MIT Press.

Brecher, R. and C. Diaz-Alejandro (1977), Tariffs, Foreign Capital and Immiserizing Growth, *Journal of International Economics*, 7, 317-322.

Brecher, R.A. and R. Findlay. (1983), Tariff, Foreign Capital and National Welfare with Sector Specific Factors, *Journal of International Economics*, 14: 277-288.

Brimble P. and C. Sripaipan, (1994) "Science and Technology Issues in Thailand Industrial Sector: The Key to the Future", Report prepared for the Asian Development Bank.

Burniaux, J. M., J. P. Mantin, G. Nicoletti, and J. O. Martins (1991a), "The Costs of Policies to Reduce Global Emissions of CO2: Initial Simulation Results with GREEN", *Working Paper No. 103, Economics and Statistics Department*, OECD, Paris, June.

Burniaux, J. M., J. P. Mantin, G. Nicoletti, and J. O. Martins (1991b), "GREEN-A Multi-Sector, Multi-region Dynamic General Equilibrium Model for Quantifying the Costs of Curbing CO_2 Emissions: A Technical Manual", *Working Paper No. 104, Economics and Statistics Department*, OECD, Paris, June.

Bulmer-Thomas, V. (1982), "Input-Output Analysis in Developing Countries", New York: John Wiley & Sons LTD.

Busse, M. (2004), 'Trade, Environmental Regulations and the World Trade Organization: New Empirical Evidence', *World Bank Policy Research, Working Paper 3361*, July.

Carraro, c. and D. Siniscalco (1992), Environmental Innovation Policy and International Competition, *Environmental and Resource Economics* 2(2): 183-200.

Chichilnisky, G. (1994), North-South Trade and the Globe Environment, *American Economic Review*, 84: 851-875.

Co, C. Y., List, J. A. and Qui, L. D. (2003), Intellectual Property Rights, Environmental Regulations and Foreign Direct Investment, *Land Economics*.

Cole, M.A. and R.J.R. Elliot (2001), 'Factor Endowments or Environmental Regulations? Determining the Trade-Environment Composition Effect', The University of Birmingham, *Department of Economics Discussion Paper 01-06*:1-38.

Cole, M.A., R.J.R. Elliott and A.K. Azhar (2001), 'The Determinants of Trade in Pollution Intensive Industries: North-South Evidence', *Working Paper, Department of Economics*, University of Birmingham.

Copeland, B. R. and M. S. Taylor (1994), North-South Trade and the Environment, *Quarterly Journal of Economics*, 109: 755-87.

Copeland, B. R. and M. Scott Taylor (1995b), Trade and Transboundary Pollution, *American Economic Review* 85(4): 716-737.

Copeland, B. R. and M. S. Taylor (1997), The Trade-Induced Degradation Hypothesis, *Resource and Energy Economics* 19 (4): 321-344.

Copeland, B.R., and M.S. Taylor (1999), Trade, Spatial Separation, and the Environment, *Journal of International Economics*, 47, 137-168.

Copeland B. R. and M. S. Taylor (2003), "Trade and the Environment: Theory and Evidence", Princeton University Press, Princeton, New Jersey USA.

Copeland B. R. and M. S. Taylor (2004), Trade, Growth and the Environment, *Journal of Economic Literature*, 42(1): 1-128.

Crandall, R. W. (1981), "Pollution Controls and Productivity Growth in Basic Industries", Cowing, T. and R. Stevenson (eds.), *Productivity Measurements in Regulated Industries*, New York: Academic Press.

Cumberland, J. D. (1979), "Inter-regional Pollution Spillovers and Consistency of Environmental Policy", in H. Siebert, ed., *Regional Environmental Policy: The Economic Issue*. New York: University Press.

Cumberland, J. D. (1981), Efficiency and Equity in Interregional Environmental Management, *Review of Regional Studies,* 2, 1-9.

Customs Department, External Account of Thailand, Various Issues.

Daly, H. E. (1993a), The Perils of Free Trade, *Scientific American,* 269: 50-57.

Daly, H. E. (1993b), "Problems with Free Trade: Neoclassical and Steady-State Perspectives", Zaelke, D. P. Orbuch and R. F. Housman (eds.), *Trade and the Environment: Law, Economics, and Policy,* Washingten, DC: Island Press.

Dasgupta, P., R. Eastwood, and G. Heal (1978), Resource Management in a Trading Economy, *Quarterly Journal of Economics* 92: 297-306.

Dasgupta, S. *et al.* (1995), "Environmental Regulation and Development: A Cross-Country Empirical Analysis". *Policy Research Working Paper No 1448.* Washington: World Bank.

Drake-Brockman, J. and K. Anderson(1994), "The Trade-Environment Debate and its Implications for Asia-Pacific", *Centre for International Economic Studies, Discussion Paper, 23* November.

D'Areg, R. (1971), "International Trade, Domestic Income, and Environmental Controls," in A. Kneese, ed., *Managing the Environment,* NY: Praeger.

De Mello, L R., Jr., (1999), Foreign Direct Investment-Led Growth Evidence from Time Series and Panel Data, *Oxford Economic Papers* 51: 133-151.

Denison, E. (1979), "Accounting for Slower Economic Growth", Washington, DC: the Brookings Institution.

Dervis, K., J. de Melo, and S. Robinson (1982), "General Equilibrium Models for Development Policy", A World Bank Research Publication. Washington, DC: The World Bank.

Dean, J, M. E. Lovely and H. Wang (2004), "Are Foreign Investors Attracted To Weak Environmental Regulations? Evaluating the Evidence from China". *World Bank USITC Working Paper 2004-01-B* May.

DEDP (1980, 1990, 2000), 'Thailand Energy Situation in 1980, 1990 and 2000', Department of Energy Development and Promotion, Thailand.

Dragun, A.K. and C. Tisdell (1999), "Sustainable Agriculture and Environment: Globalization and the Impact of Trade Liberalization", Northampton, MA: Edward Elgar Publishing.

Durbin, A. (1995), Trade and the Environment: The North-South Divide, *Environment* 37(7): 16-24.

Edmonds, J., S. H. Kim, C. N. McCracken, R. D. Sands, and M. A. Wise (1997). "Return to 1990: The Cost of Mitigating United States Carbon Emissions in the Post-2000 Period", Washington, D.C.: Pacific Northwest National Laboratory Operated by Battelle Memorial Institute, October.

EPA Trade and Environment Committee (1991), Minutes of Aug. 5, Meeting, Aug. 6.

ESCAP/UNCTAD (1997), Competitive Business Strategies of Asian Transnational Corporations, New York: United Nations.

Eskeland, G.S. & A.E. Harrison (2003), Moving to Greener Pastures? Multinationals and Pollution Haven Hypothesis, *Journal of Development Economics*,70(1): 1-23.

Forsund, F. R., (1985), "Input-Output Models, National Economic Models, and the Environment," Handbook of Natural Resource and Energy Economics, in: A. V. Kneese & J. L. Sweeney (ed.), *Handbook of Natural Resource and Energy Economics*, Edition 1, Volume 1, Chapter 8: 325-341.

Forssell, O. & Polenske, K. R. (1998), Introduction in Input-Output and the Environment, *Economic Systems Research*, 10: 91-97.

Frankel, J and A. Rose (2001), Is Trade Good or Bad for the Environment? Sorting out the Causality, *NBER Working Paper Series, 9201* September.

French H. F. (1993), Costly Tradeoffs: Reconciling Trade and the Environment, *Worldwatch Paper #113*, Worldwatch Institute, Washington, D.C,USA.

Friedman, J., D. Gerlowski, and J. Silberman. (1992), What Attracts Foreign Multinational Corporations? Evidence from Branch Plant Location in the United States. *Journal of Regional Science* 32: 403-418.

Gale, I. V. and R. Lewis (1995), Trade Liberalization and Pollution: An Input-Output Study of Carbon Dioxide Emissions in Mexico, *Economic Systems Research*, 7(3): 309-320.

Gerilla, G. and Kagawa, P. and Inamura, H. (2002). International Trade and Carbon Emissions: A Case of China and Japan. Paper presented at the 14th International Conference on

Input-Output Techniques held at UQAM Montreal Canada October 10–15.

Glomsrod, S., H. Vennemo, and T. Johnson (1992), Stablization of Emissions of CO_2: A Computable General Equilibrium Assessment, *Scandinavian Journal of Economics* 94 (1): 53-69.

Gray, W. and R. Shadbegian (1997), 'Environmental Regulation, Investment Timing, and Technology Choice', *Centre for Economic Studies, US-WP-97-9*, July.

Grossman, G. M & E. Helpman, (1995), Trade Wars and Trade Talks, *Journal of Political Economy*, 103(4):675-708, August.

Grossman, G.M. and A.B. Krueger. (1995), Economic Growth and the Environment, *Quarterly Journal of Economics* 110(2): 353-377, May.

Grossman, G.M. and A.B. Krueger. (1993), 'Environmental Impacts of a North American Free Trade Agreement'. in P.M. Garber. (ed) *The Mexico-U.S. Free Trade Agreement*, 13-56. Cambridge, Massachusetts and London: MIT Press.

Haan, de M., (2002), Extending the Scope of Environmental Indicators by Taking into Account International Trade Dependencies, Paper presented at the 14th International Conference on Input-Output Techniques held at UQAM, Montreal, Canada, 10-15 October.

Hayami, H and M. Nakamura (2002), 'CO2 Emission of Alternative Technologies and Bilateral Trade between Japan and Canada: Relocating Production and an Implication for Joint Implementation', Keio Economic Observatory, *Discussion Paper 75, Keio University*, Japan: 1-34.

Hazilla, M. and R. J. Kopp (1990), Social Cost of Environmental Quality Regulations: A General Equilibrium Analysis, *Journal of Political Economy* 98: 853-73.

Hettige, H., R. E. B. Lucas, and D. Wheeler (1992), The Toxic Intensity of Industrial Production: Global Pattern, Trends and Trade Policy, *American Economic Review Papers and Proceedings* 82: 478-481.

Hettige, H., P. Martin, M. Singh and D.R. Wheeler (1995), 'The Industrial Pollution Projection System'. Policy *Research Working Paper 1431, Washington, World Bank.*

Henriques, I, and P. Sadorsky (1996), The Determinants of an Environmentally Responsive Firm: An Empirical Approach, *Journal of Environmental Economics and Management*, 30 (3), 381-395.

Hopkins, T. D. (1992), "Regulation and Jobs-Sorting Out the Consequences", Prepared for the American Petroleum Institute, Washington, DC, October.

Housman, R. and D. Zaelke (1992), Trade, Environment, and Sustainable Development: A Primer, *Hastings International and Comparative Law Review*, 15(4): 535-612.

Hudson, S. (1993), 'Trade, Environment and the Pursuit of Sustainable Development", McAlpine, J. C. and P. Le Donne eds, *The Greening of World Trade, A Report to EPA* from EPA Trade and Environment Committee, Printed by the US Government Printing Office.

Ierland, E. C. (1993), 'Macroeconomic Analysis of Environmental Policy', Amsterdam: Elsevier.

International Monetary Fund—International Financial Statistics, Various Issues.

Jackson, J. H. (1992), World Trade Rules and Environmental Policies: Congruence or Conflict?, *Washington and Lee Law Review*, 49 (4): 1227-78.

Jaffe, A. B., S. R. Peterson, P. R. Portney, and P. N. Stavins (1995), Environmental regulation and the Competitiveness of US Manufacturing: What Does the Evidence Tell Us? *Journal of Economic Literature* 33, 132-163.

Jaffe, A. B., & K. Palmer, (1997) Environmental Regulation and Innovation: A Panel Data Study, *The Review of Economics and Statistics*, 79(4): 610-619, November.

Jenkins, R., Barton, J., Bartzokas, A., Hesselberg, J., Knutsen, J.M. (2002), 'Environmental Regulation in the New Global Economy', Cheltenham, UK: Edward Elgar Publishing Limited.

Jha, V, A. Markandya and R. Vossenaar(1999), 'Reconciling Trade and Environment : Lessons from Case Studies in Developing Countries', *Trade Environment and Development Section (UNCTAD)*, Geneva, Edward Elgar, Cheltenham, U.K. Northampton, MA, USA.

Johnstone, N. (1997), "Globalization, Technology, and Environment." *Globalization and Environment,* OECD Proceedings, OECD: Paris.

Jorgenson, D.W and P.J. Wilcoxen (1990), Intertemporal General Equilibrium Modeling of U.S. Environmental Regulation, *Journal of Policy Modeling,* 12 (4): 715-744.

Jorgenson, D. W and P. J. Wilcoxen (1993), "Energy, the Environment, and Economic Growth", Kneese, A. V. and J. L. Sweeney (eds.), *Handbook of Natural Resource and Energy Economics* Vol. III, Amsterdam: Elsevier.

Kalt, J. P. (1989), Exhaustible Resource, Price Policy, International Trade, and Intertemporal Welfare, *Journal of Environmental Economics and Management*, 17(2):109-26.

Kanittha, I. (1996), Levels of Pollution Remain Stagnant, *Bangkok Post*, December 31,: 1-3.

Kohpaiboon, A. (2003), Foreign Trade Regimes and the FDI-Growth Nexus: A Case Study of Thailand, *The Journal of Development Studies*, 40(2): 55-69.

Kolstad C. & Y. Xing, (1998), 'Do Lax Environmental Regulations Attract Foreign Investment?,' University of California at Santa Barbara, Economics *Working Paper Series 1078,* Department of Economics, UC Santa Barbara.

Kritayakirana, K. *et al.* (1989), 'The Development of Thailand's Technological Capability in Industry'. Six volumes, Bangkok: Thailand Development Research Institute.

Krishna Kumar, T. (2005), Economic Growth and Productivity Gains from Capital Inflows: a Reply, *Journal of Quantitative Economics*, 3(1): 161-63 New Series, January.

Krutilla, K. (1991), Environmental Regulation in an Open Economy, *Journal of Environmental Economics and Management*, 20(2): 127-42.

Lange, G.M., (1998), Applying an Integrated Natural Resource Accounts and Input-Output Model to Development Planning in Indonesia, *Economic Systems Research*, 10 (2), 113-134.

Lange, G. M., and R. Hassan, (2002), Trade and the Environment in Southern Africa: The Impact of the 'User Pays' Principle for Water on Exports of Botswana, Namibia, and South Africa. Paper presented at the 14th International Conference on Input-Output Techniques held at UQAM, Montreal, Canada, 10–15 October.

Leamer, E. E. (1984), "Sources of International Comparative Advantage: Theory and Evidence", Cambridge: MIT Press.

Leamer, E. E. (1980), The Leontief Paradox Reconsidered, *Journal of Political Economy* 88: 495-503.

Leamer, E. E. and J. Levinsohn (1995), "International Trade Theory: The Evidence", Grossman, G. M. and K. Rogoff (eds.), *Handbook of International Economics*, Vol. III, Amsterdam: Elsevier.

Letchumanan, R. and F. Kodama (2000), Reconciling the Conflict between the Pollution-Havens Hypothesis and an Emerging Trajectory of International Technology Transfer, *Research Policy*, 29: 59-79.

Leonard, H. J. and C. J. Duerksen (1980), Environmental Regulations and the Location of Industry: An International Perspective, *Columbia Journal of World Business:* 52-68.

Leonard, H. J. (1988), 'Pollution and the Struggle for the World Product'. NY: Cambridge.

Leontief. W (1951), 'The Structure of American Economy, 1919-39', Second Edition, Oxford University Press, New York.

Leontief. W (1966), Input-Output Economics, Oxford University Press, New York.

Leontief, W.W. (1970), Environmental Repercussions and the Economic Structure: An Input-Output Approach, *The Review of Economics and Statistics* 52: 262-271.

Leontief, W.W. (1973), "National Income, Economic Structure, and Environmental Externalities", in M. Moss (ed.) *The Measurement of Economic and Social Performance, Studies in Income and Wealth*, 38, New York: National Bureau of Economic Research.

Leontief, W., A. Carter, and P. Petri. (1977), "Future of the World Economy". New York: Oxford University Press.

Leontief, W.W. and D. Ford (1972), "Air Pollution and the Economic Structure: Empirical Results of Input-Output

Computations", in A. Brody and A.P. Carter (eds.), *Input-Output Techniques*, Amsterdam: North-Holland.

Lenzen, M. and J. Munksgaard, (2002), Energy and Greenhouse Gas Emissions Embodied in Trade, Paper presented at the 14th International Conference on Input-Output Techniques held at UQAM, Montreal, Canada, 10-15 October.

Levinson, A. (1996), Environmental Regulations and Manufacturers Location Choices, Evidence from the Census of Manufacturers, *Journal of Public Economics* 62:5-29.

Li, Jennifer C. (2005), Is There a Trade-Off between Trade Liberalization and Environmental Quality? A CGE Assessment on Thailand, *The Journal of Environment & Development*, 14(2): 252-277.

Liddle, B. (2001), Free Trade and the Environment-Development System, *Ecological Economics*, 39(1):21-36.

Limanon, W., (1999), 'Thai Industrial Environmental Performance Rating Program: Using Public Disclosure to Reduce Emissions from Industrial Estates'. Masters thesis, George Washington University Law School, Washington, D.C.

Lipsey, R.E., (2000), Inward FDI and Economic Growth in Developing Countries, *Transnational Corporations, 9(1): 67-95.*

List, J.A. (2001), U.S. Country-Level Determinants of Inbound FDI: Evidence from a Two-Step Modified Count Data Model, *International Journal of Industrial Organization*, 19, 6: 953-973.

List, J.A. and C.Y. Co. (1999), The Effects of Environmental Regulations on Foreign Direct Investment, *Journal of Environmental Economics and Management,* 40: 1-20.

Lopez, R. (1994), The Environment as a Factor of Production: The Effects of Economic Growth and Trade Liberalization, *Journal of Environmental Economics and Management*, 27(2), 163-84.

Low, P and A. Yeats (1992), 'Do Dirty Industries Migrate?' In P. Low (Ed.), *International Trade and the Environment (World Bank Discussion Paper #159)* Washington, DC: World Bank: 89-104.

Lucas, R., D. Wheeler and H. Hettige (1992), 'Economic Development, Environmental Regulation, and International Migration of Toxic Industrial Pollution: 1960-1988', In P. Low (Ed.), *International Trade and the Environment (World Bank Discussion Paper #159),* Washington, DC: World Bank: 67-88.

Lucas, R.E.B., D. Wheeler, and H. Hettige. (1990), 'Economic Development, Environmental Regulation and the International Migration of Toxic Industrial Pollution'. Paper presented at the *Symposium on* International *Trade and the Environment*, Washington D.C.

Machado. G, R. Schaeffer and E. Worrell (2001), Energy and Carbon Embodied in the International Trade of Brazil: An Input-Output Approach, *Ecological Economics*, 39(3): 409-424.

Maestad, O. (1998), On the Efficiency of Green Trade Policy, *Environmental and Resource Economics* 11(1): 1-18.

Magee, S., and W.F. Ford (1972), Environmental Pollution, the Terms of Trade, and the Balance of Payments of the United States, *Kyklos* 25, 101-18.

Manne, A. S. (1992), "Global 2100: Alternative Scenarios for Reducing Carbon Emissions", *Working Papers No. 111*, Department of Economics and Statistics, OECD, Paris.

Manne, A. S. and R. G. Richels (1991a), Global CO2 Emission Reductions—the Impacts of Rising Energy Costs, *The Energy Journal,* 12 (1): 87-107.

Manne, A. S. and R. G. Richels (1991b), International Trade in Carbon Emission Rights: A Decomposition Procedure, *American Economic Review* 81 (2): 135-139.

Manne, A. S. and R. G. Richels (1992), 'Buying Greenhouse Insurance: The Economic Costs of CO2 Emission Limits', Cambridge, MA: The MIT Press.

Manne, A.S. and R. Richels (1996), The Berlin Mandate: The Cost of Meeting Post-2000 Targets and Timetables, *Energy Policy* 24(3), 205-210.

Mani, M. and D.Wheeler (1998), In Search of Pollution Havens? Dirty Industry in the World Economy, 1960-1995, *Journal of Environment and Development*, 7(3):215-47.

Mani, M., S. Pargal, and M. Huq. (1997), 'Does Environmental Regulation Matter? Determinants of the Location of New Manufacturing Plants in India'. *Policy Research Working Paper* # 1718. Washington, D.C.: The World Bank.

Markusen, J. (1975), International Externalities and Optimal Tax Structures, *Journal of International Economics*, 5, 15-29.

Markusen, J. (1997), Costly Pollution Abatement, Competitiveness, and Plant Location Decisions, *Resource and Energy Economics* 19, 299-320.

McGuire, M. (1982), Regulation, Factor Rewards, and International Trade, *Journal of Public Economics* 17: 335-354.

Meadous, D., D. Meadows, J. Randers and W. W. Behrens III (1972), 'Limits to Growth', New York: Universe Books.

Merrifield, J. (1988), The Impact of Selected Abatement Strategies on Transnational Pollution, the Terms of Trade, and Factor Rewards: a General Equilibrium Approach, *Journal of Environmental Economics and Management*, 15, 259-284.

Melvin, J. R. (1968), Production and Trade with Two Factor and Three Goods, *American Economic Review* 63: 1249-1268.

MOSTE (1997), Ministry of Science, Technology and Environment, Thailand Policy and Prospective Plan for Enhancement and Conservation of National Environmental Quality, 1997-2016, *Office of the Environmental Policy and Planning*, Bangkok, Thailand, December.

Mukhopadhyay, K. (2004), Environmental Impacts of Trade with Europe: A Study on the Impact of Trade with EU on CO_2 Emissions in India during 1990s, *IDPAD Newsletter, II* (1):27-34.

Mukhopadhyay, K and D. Chakraborty (2005a), Environmental Impacts of Trade in India, *International Trade Journal*, 19(2): 135-163.

Mukhopadhyay, K. and D. Chakraborty (2005b), Is Free Trade Good for the Environment? Evidence from India, *Asia Pacific Development Journal, 12(1):109-136.*

Mukhopadhyay, K and O. Forssell (2005), An Empirical Investigation of Air Pollution from Fossil Fuel Combustion and its Impact on Health in India during 1973–1974 to 1996–1997, *Ecological Economics,* 55(2): 235-250.

Munksgaard, J. and K.A. Pedersen (2001), CO_2 Accounts for Open Economies: Producer or Consumer Responsibility? *Energy Policy*, 29(4): 327-35.

Mulatu, A, Raymond J.G.M. Florax and C. Withagen (2004), 'Environmental Regulation and International Trade: Empirical Results for Germany, the Netherlands and the US, 1977-1992', *Contributions to Economic Analysis & Policy, The B.E. Journals in Economic Analysis & Policy*, 3(2) *Article* 5.

Murrell, P. (1990), "The Nature of Socialist Economics: Lessons from East European Foreign Trade", Princeton University Press, USA.

Mutti John H. and J.D. Richardson (1977), International Competitive Displacements from Environmental Controls: The Quantitative Gains from Methodological Refinement, *Journal of Environmental Economics and Management*, 4(2):135-152.

Myers C.N. and C. Sussangkarn, (1992), Educational Options for the Future of Thailand: Summary of the Synthesis of Research Findings, *TDRI Quarterly Review* 7(1), March.

NESDB (2002), Capital Stock of Thailand, National Economic and Social Development Board publication, Office of the Prime Minister, Bangkok, Thailand.

NESDB (2004), Report on Thailand Industrial Performance, National Economic and Social Development Board publication, Office of the Prime Minister, Bangkok, Thailand.

NESDB (2005), Thailand Economic Performance and Outlook, National Economic and Social Development Board publication, Office of the Prime Minister, Bangkok, Thailand.

NESDB (1984, 1994, 2004), Input –Output Tables of Thailand for the year 1980, 1990, 2000, Office of the Prime Minister, Bangkok, Thailand.

NESDB (2003), National Income of Thailand, 1980-2001 edition, Office of the Prime Minister, Bangkok, Thailand.

NESDB (1998), "Indicators of Well being and Policy Analysis", Newsletter of National Economic and Social Development Board's Development Evaluation Division, (February, March and May).

N.S.O. (1981, 1991, 2001,2003), Report of the Labour Force Survey Whole Kingdom, National Statistical Office Publication Office of the Prime Minister, Bangkok, Thailand.

N.S.O. (1981, 1991), Report of the Industrial Survey Whole Kingdom-National Statistical Office Publication, Office of the Prime Minister, Bangkok, Thailand.

N.S.O. (2001), Report of the Manufacturing Industrial Survey Whole Kingdom-National Statistical Office Publication, Office of the Prime Minister, Bangkok, Thailand.

Oates, W. E. and R. M. Schwab (1988), Economic Competition among Jurisdiction Efficiency Enhancing or Distortion Inducing?, *Journal of Public Economics* 35: 333-354.

OECD (1986), Department of Economics and Statistics, Foreign Trade by Commodities, Export and Import, Volume I & II, 1984, Organization for Economic Co-operation and Development, Paris.

——(1992, 2002), Foreign Trade by Commodities, Statistics Directorate 1990 & (1996/2001), Volume 5, Organization for Economic Co-Operation and Development, Paris.

OECD (1982), Macro-Economic Evaluation of Environmental Programmes, Paris.

OECD (1985), The Macro-Economic Impact of Environmental Expenditure, OECD Publications, Printed in Paris.

OECD, (1996), Organization for Economic Cooperation and Development. Reconciling Trade, Environment and Development Policies. Paris.

OECD (1994), The Environmental Effects of Trade, OECD Publications, Printed in Paris.

OECD (1997), Freight and the Environment: Effects of Trade Liberalisation and Transport Sector Reforms, Environment Directorate, Organisation for Economic Co-operation and Development (OECD), Paris.

Paitoonpong, S & S. Abe (2004), *The Thai Economy: A Picture from the Past, TDRI Report,* 19(4): 3-12.

Palmer K. L., Wallace E. Oates, and Paul R. Portney (1995), Tightening Environmental Standards: The Benefit-Cost or the No-Cost Paradigm? *Journal of Economic Perspectives*, 9:119-132.

Panayotou, T. (1997), Demystifying the Environmental Kuznets Curve: Turning a Black Box into a Policy Tool, *Environmental and Development Economics*, 2(4): 465-484.

Panayotou, T., T. Schatzki and Q. Limvorapitak. (1997), "Differential Industry Response to Formal and Informal Environmental Regulations in Newly Industrializing Economies: The Case of Thailand." A Case Study for the HIID Asia Environmental Economics Policy Seminar.

Pargal, S. and D. Wheeler (1996), Informal Regulation of Industrial Pollution in Developing Countries: Evidence from Indonesia, *Journal of Political Economy* 104(6).

Park, S.H. and W.C. Labys (1999), 'Industrial Development and Environmental Degradation: A Source Book on the Origins of Global Pollution', Northampton, MA: Edward Elgar.

Pasurka, C. A. (1984), The Short run Impact of Environmental Protection Costs on US Product Prices, *Journal of Environmental Economics and Management* 11: 380-90.

Phantumvanit, D.; Wigzell, S; Buranakul, E.; Bootherawara, N.; Bowonwiwat, R. (1994), 'The Interlinkages Between Trade and Environment': Thailand. Report prepared for the United Nations Conference on Trade and Development, Geneva, Switzerland; Thailand Environment Institute, Bangkok, Thailand. 175.

PCD (1994), 'Pollution Control Department', Pollution Control Report, Singapore: Environmental Policy and Management Division, Ministry of the Environment.

Pearson, C. (1987), 'Multinational Corporations, Environment, and the Third World'. Durham: Duke University Press.

Patmasiriwat D., Kuik O. and Pednekar S., (1999),'Shrimp Aquaculture Sector in Thailand: A Review of Economic, Environmental and Trade Issues, The Free to Non-OECD Countries', Environmental Publications from UNEP and Key International Organisations, Earth Print Ltd, Hertfordshire, England.

Perroni, C. and R. M. Wigle (1994), International Trade and Environment Quality: How Important are the Linkages? *Canadian Journal of Economics*, XXVII (3): 551-67.

Pethig, R. (1976), Pollution, Welfare and Environmental Policy in the Theory of Comparative Advantage, *Journal of Environmental Economics and Management*, 2:160-169.

Petri, P. A. (1976), "A Multilateral Model of Japanese-American Trade", Polenske, K. R. and J. V. Skolka (eds.), *Advances in Input-Output Analysis*, Cambridge: Ballinger Publishing Company.

Phongpaichit, P and C. Baker (2002), 'Thailand Economy and Politics', Second Edition, Oxford University Press, New York.

Porter, M. E. and C. Van der Linde (1995), Toward a New Conception of the Environment-Competitiveness Relationship, *Journal of Economic Perspectives* 9:97-118.

Proops, J.L., G.Atkinson, B.F.V .Schlotheim and S, Simon (1999), International Trade and the Sustainability Footprint: A Practical Criterion for its Assessment, *Ecological Economics*, 28(1): 75-97.

Przybylinski, M., (2002), Bilateral "Pollution Flows" between Poland and Germany, Paper presented at the 14th International Conference on Input-Output Techniques held at UQAM, Montreal, Canada, 10-15 October.

Pupphavesa, W and B. Pussarungsri (1994), 'FDI in Thailand', International Economic Relations Program, *TDRI Report*, April.

Puttock, G. D. and M. Sabourin (1992), "International Trade in Forest Products: An Overview", International Agricultural Trade Research Consortium, St. Petersburg, Fl.

Ratanalangkorn, T. and Padungcheevit, W. (1995), "The Role of Monetary Policy and Fiscal Policies in Solving the Problems of Poverty and Income Distribution" Papers on Policy Analysis and Assessment, Economic Research Department, Bank of Thailand.

Rauscher, M. (1991), "Foreign Trade and the Environment", Siebert, H. eds., *Environmental Scarcity; The International Dimension*, Institut Fuer Weltwirtschaft an der Universitaet Kiel, Tuebingen: Mohr.

Robison, H.D. (1988), Industrial Pollution Abatement: The Impact on the Balance of Trade, *Canadian Journal of Economics* 21(1).

Rock, M.T. (2002), 'Pollution Control in East Asia: Lessons from Newly Industrializing Economies', Resources for the Future, Washington D.C.

Rose, A., M. M. Tompkins, D. Lim, O. Frias, and J. Benavides (1994), "Coal Use in the People's Republic of China", Vol. 2: The Economic Effects of Constraining Coal Utilization, ANL/DIS/TM-22, Argonne National Laboratory, Argonne, Illinois.

Runge, C. F. (1990), Trade Protectionism and Environmental Regulations: The New Non-tariff Barriers, *Northwestern Journal of International Law & Business*, 11(1): 47-61.

Runge, C.F. (1993), "Economic Trade and Environmental Protection" in J. Braden, H. Folmer and T. Ulen (eds.) *Environmental Policy with Economic and Political Integration: The European Community and the United States*, Edward Elgar.

Saunders, J.O. (1994), NAFTA and the North American Agreement on Environmental Cooperation: A New Model for International Collaboration on Trade and the Environment, *Colorado Journal of International Environmental Law and Policy*, 5 (2): 273-304.

Scherr, S. J. (1987), "Hazardous Exports: US and International Policy Developments," in C. Pearson, Multinational Corporations, Environment, and the Third World. Durham: Duke Univ. Press.

Schneider, K, and D. Wellisch (1997), Eco-Dumping, Capital Mobility, and International Trade, *Environmental and Resource Economics,* 10: 387-404.

Selden, T. M. and D. Song (1994), Environmental Quality and Development: Is there a Kuznets Curve for Air Pollution Emissions? *Journal of Environmental Economics and Management* 27: 147-162.

Siam Walla, A, Y. Vajragupta and P.Yanond (1999), Foreign Capital Flows to Thailand: Determinants and Impact, *TDRI Report*, November.

Siebert, H. (1977), Environmental Quality and the Gains from Trade, *Kyklos*, 30(4): 657-673.

Siebert, H., J. Eichberger, R. Gronych, and R. Pethig (1980), 'Trade and Environment: A Theoretical Enquiry', Elsevier Scientific Publishing Company, New York.

Sinn, H. W. (1994), How Much Europe? Subsidiarity, Centralization and Fiscal Competition, *Scottish Journal of Political Economy,* 41: 85-107.

Smarzynska, B. K., and S.J. Wei (2004), Pollution Haven and Foreign Direct Investment: Dirty Secret or Popular Myth? Contributions to Economic Analysis & Policy, *The B.E. Journals in Economic Analysis & Policy* 3(2), Article 8.

Smith, B. and A. Ulph (1982), "The Impact of Environmental Policies in Developed Countries on the Trade of the Developing Countries," *Environment and Development in Asia and the Pacific*, UNEP Reports and Proceedings Series 6, Nairobi.

Snape, W. (1994), Searching for GATT's Environmental Miranda: Are 'Process Standard' Getting Due Process? *Cornell International Law Journal*, 27(3): 777-815.

Stokes, B. (1992), On the Brink, *National Journal* 29 (Feb): 504-509.

Stewart, R.B. (1993), Environmental Regulation and International Competitiveness, *Yale Law Journal*, June, 102(8): 2039-2106.

Suh, S., (2004), CEDA 3.0 (Comprehensive Environmental Data Archive): Environmental Input-Output Database for the United States, Institute of Environmental Sciences (CML), Leiden University, Leiden, the Netherlands.

Suh, S., (2005), Developing Sectoral Environmental Database for Input-Output Analysis: Comprehensive Environmental Data Archive of the U.S., *Economic Systems Research*, 17 (4), 449–469.

Symons, E. J., J. L. R. Proops and P. W. Gay (1990), 'Carbon Taxes, Consumer Demand and Carbon Dioxide Emission: A Simulation Analysis for the UK' Department of Economics and Mangement Science, University of Keele, Staffs.

Tangkitvanich, S. *et al.*, (2004) 'Thailand' Chapter 7 in Brook, D.H. and H. Hill edited *Managing FDI in a Globalizing Economy-Asian Experience*, Palgrave McMilan, ADB.

Tay J. (1993), 'Environmental Protection in Singapore': *Working Paper*. Singapore Nanyang Technical University.

Tesco, C. (1993), 'Main Report on Management of Environment in Thailand and Operation Plan for Bangkok Metropolitan Region', Report Submitted to The Ministry of Science Technology and Environment.

TDRI (2000), 'The State of Environment in Thailand: A Decade of Change', edited by Kaosa-ard, M and, P Wijukprasert, *Natural Resources and Environment Program*, Thailand Development Research Institute Publication, Bangkok, Thailand.

TDRI (1996), 'Environmental Strategy for Thailand, *Natural Resources and Environment Program*', Thailand Development Research Institute Publication, Bangkok, Thailand, September.

TEI (2000), 'The Compatibility of International Trade and Environmental Regulation: Implications for Thailand and Other Developing Nations', Thailand Environment Institute Report, April, Thailand.

TEI (1997), 'A Study on Industrial Pollution and Pollution Abatement Equipment in Thailand', Project Report prepared for DIW, Thailand.

Tinakorn, P. (1992), "Industrialization and Welfare: How Poverty and Income Distribution are Affected", Paper presented at the Conference on the Making of a Fifth Tiger? Thailand's Industrialization and its Consequences, Australian National University, 7-9 December.

TISI (2000), ISO 14000 Certification: Tally and Details, Thailand Industrial Standards Institute, Bangkok.

Tobey, J.A. (1990), The Effects of Domestic Environmental Policies, *Kyklos*, 43(2): 191-209.

Tobey, J. A. (1993), "Effects of Domestic Environmental Policy on Patterns of International Trade", Shane, M. D. and H. van Witzke eds., The Environment, Government Policies, and International Trade: A Proceedings, USDA: Staff Report No. AGES 9314.

Torii, Y., S. J. Shim, and Y. Akiyama (1989), "Effects of Tariff Reductions on Trade in the Asia-Pacific Region", Miller, R. E., K. R. Polenske, and A. Z. Rose (eds.), *Frontiers of Input-Output Analysis*, Oxford: Oxford University Press.

Townsend, B and R. Ratnayake (2000), "Trade Liberalization and the Environment", World Scientific Publishing Co., Singapore.

Trefler, D. (1994), "The Case of the Missing Trade and Other HOV Mysteries", University of Toronto, mimeo.

Ulph, A. and L. Valentini (1997), Plant Location and Strategic Environmental Policy with Intersectoral Linkages, *Resource and Energy Economics* 19(4): 363-383.

U. S. Environmental Protection Agency (1992), "The Clean Air Market Place: New Business Opportunities Created by the Clean Air Act Amendments—Summary of Conference Proceedings", Washington, D. C., Office of Air and Radiation, July 24, 1992.

United Nations (1984, 1992, 2001), 'Yearbook of International Trade Statistics' Department of Economic and Social Affairs, Vol-I, UN publication, New York.

UNCTAD (2001), 'FDI in Least Developed Countries at a Glance', UNCTAD Report.

UNCTAD (2002), 'Asia-Pacific FDI Inflows', TAD/INF/PR/51, UNCTAD Press Release.

UNCTAD (2003), "Environmental Goods: Trade Statistics of Developing Countries",TD/B/COM.1/EM.21/CRP.1, Geneva, http://r0.unctad.org/trade_env/test1/meetings/egs/crp.pdf?docID=3187%2B%22ItemID=2068).

UN (1996), 'Key Issues in Trade and Environment Debate', E/CN.17/1996/IDC/Misc.1, Department of Economic and Social Affairs, Division for Sustainable Development New York, USA.

UN (1995), 'Trade, Environment and Sustainable Development', E/CN.17/1995/12, Department of Economic and Social Affairs, Division for Sustainable Development, New York, USA.

UN (2003), 'Trade and Environment', United Nations Publication.

UNCTAD/UNDP (1994), 'The Inter-linkages between Trade and Environment', Geneva, Final report, June.

UNCTAD (2006), 'Trade and Environment Review', UNCTAD Geneva.

UNEP (2005), 'Environment and Trade: A Handbook', The United Nations Environment Programme, Published by the International Institute for Sustainable Development, Division of Technology, Industry and Economics, Economics and Trade Branch, second edition, Geneva, Switzerland.

UNIDO (2002), 'Tracking Manufacturing Performance: A Review of the Industrial Sector in Thailand', UNIDO *Integrated Programme for Thailand-Component 6, Occasional paper series*, United Nations Industrial Development Organisation.

Van der Linden, J. A. and J. Oosterhaven (1995), European Community Inter-country Input-Output Relations: Construction Method and Main Results for 1965-85, *Economic Systems Research*, 7(3): 249-70.

Vanek, J. (1968), The Factor Proportions Theory: the n-Factor Case, *Kyklos* 21: 749-756.

Wadeskog, A. (2002), 'Trade and the Environment in Input-Output Based Environmentally Accounts Analysis', Paper presented at the 14th International Conference on Input-Output Techniques held at UQAM, Montreal, Canada 10-15th October.

Waldkirch, A. and M. Gopinath (2004) 'Pollution Haven or Hythe? New Evidence from Mexico' *International Trade 0412005, Economics Working Paper Archive at WUSTL*: 1-34.

Walter, I. (1973), The Pollution Content of American Trade, *Western Economic Journal* 11, 61-70.

Walter, I. (1982), "Environmentally Induced Industrial Relocation to Developing Countries," in S. Rubin, ed., Environmental Trade. New Jersey: Allanheld, Osmum, and Co., 67-101.

Warr, P. (1999), 'Thailand: Trade shocks and Domestic Responses'. In P Collier and J Gunning and Associates, *Trade Shocks in Developing Countries,* Oxford, Clarendon Press, Second Volumes, 201-232.

WCED (1987), 'Our Common Future, World Commission on Environment and Development', Oxford University Press, New York.

Wellisch, D. (1995), Locational Choices of Firms and Decentralized Environmental Policy with Various Instruments, *Journal of Urban Economics* 37, 290-310.

Wheeler, D. and A. Mody (1992), International Investment Location Decisions: The Case of US Firms, *Journal of International Economics,* 33: 57-76.

Wheeler, D. (2000), 'Racing to the Bottom? Foreign Investment and Air Pollution in Developing Countries'. *Policy Research Working Paper* #2524. Washington, D.C.: The World Bank.

Whalley, J. (1991), The Interface between Environmental and Trade Policies, *Economic Journal* 101, 180-189.

Whalley, J. and R. Wigle (1991), Cutting CO2 Emissions: The Effects of Alternative Policy Approaches, *The Energy Journal*, 12(1).

Withagen, C. (1985), 'Economic Theory and International Trade in Exhaustible Resources', Berlin: Springer-Verlag.

Wibulsawadi and Vongthieres (1994), "Strengthening the Domestic Financial System," in *The Political Economy of Policy Reform*. Washington, DC.

World Bank. (1994), "Chile: Managing Environmental Problems. Economic Analysis of Selected Issues." *Report No. 13061-CH,* Washington D. C.

World Bank (1994a), 'Thailand: Mitigating Pollution and Congestion in a High Growth Economy', *Report 11770-TH*. Washington, D.C.: World Bank.

World Bank (1992), World Development Report 1992, New York: Oxford University Press.

World Bank (2000), 'Global Economic Prospects and the Developing Countries', Washington, D.C.,

World Bank (2002), 'Thailand Economic Monitor', Washington D.C.

World Bank, (2000a), 'Thailand Environmental Monitor'. Washington D.C.

Wright, D.J. (1974), 'Goods and Services: An Input -Output Analysis', *Energy Policy*, 2(4): 307-15.

WTO (1999), 'Trade and Environment', Special Studies, No. 4, World Trade Organization, Geneva, 1999.

Wyckoff, A.W., and J.M. Roop (1994), The Embodiment of Carbon in Imports of Manufactured Products: Implications for International Agreements on Greenhouse Gas Emissions, *Energy Policy*, 22(3): 187-94.

Xing, Y. and C. D. Kolstad (1996), "Environment and Trade: A Review of Theory and Issues," University of California Santa Barbara, Department of Economics, *Working Paper #2-96*, Santa Barbara, CA.

Xing,Y and C. Kolstad (2002), Do Lax Environmental Regulations Attract Foreign Investment? *Environmental and Resource Economics*, 21(1): 1-22.

Xu, X. (1999), 'International Trade and Environmental Regulation: A Dynamic Perspective', Huntington, New York: Nova Science Publishers, Inc.

Xu, B., (2000), Multinational Enterprises, Technology Diffusion, and Host Country Productivity Growth, *Journal of Development Economics*, 62: 477-93.

Yao, Y. *et al.* (1994), 'Outlook for China Economic and Social Development', Two Volumes, Institute of Quantitative and Technical Economics, Chinese Academy of Social Science, Beijing.

Yohe, G. W. (1979), The Backward Incidence of Pollution Control—Some Comparative Statistics in General Equilibrium, *Journal of Environmental Economics and Management* 6: 187-198.

Zhang Z. X. (1998), Macroeconomic Effects of CO_2 Emission Limits: A Computable General Equilibrium Analysis for China, *Journal of Policy Modeling*, 20(2): 213-250.

Index